Peace Won by the Saber:

The Crimean War, 1853-1856

While every precaution has been taken in the preparation of this book, the publisher assumes no responsibility for errors or omissions, or for damages resulting from the use of the information contained herein.

PEACE WON BY THE SABER: THE CRIMEAN WAR, 1853-1856

First edition. January 14, 2022.

Copyright © 2022 History Nerds and Aleksa Vučković.

ISBN: 979-8215993149

Written by History Nerds and Aleksa Vučković.

Also by History Nerds

Celtic History
Ireland

Great Wars of the World
World War 1
World War 2
The Napoleonic Wars: One Shot at Glory
The Serbian Revolution: 1804-1835
Peace Won by the Saber: The Crimean War, 1853-1856
The Wars of the Roses

Irish Heroes
Grace O'Malley: The Pirate Queen of Ireland
William Butler Yeats: Nobel Prize Winning Poet
Scáthach
Finn McCool

The History of the Vikings

Vikings
Longships on Restless Seas

The Rise and Fall of Empires
Rome: The Rise and Fall

Standalone
The History of the United Kingdom
The History of Ireland
The History of America
Stalin
The Fiery Maelstrom of Freedom
The History of Scotland
Robert the Bruce
William Wallace: Scotland's Great Freedom Fighter
The History of Wales

Also by Aleksa Vučković

Great Wars of the World
Peace Won by the Saber: The Crimean War, 1853-1856

Table of Contents

Introduction

In those decades of slow recovery, in which Europe was gradually getting back on its feet from the debilitating effects of the Napoleonic Wars, the world was making bold steps towards the modern times. Napoleon was defeated once and for all in 1815, and died just a few years later in 1821. His legacy has been grim – Europe suffered immensely in an all-out war that claimed millions of lives. Such a great loss required a long period of recovery – one that Europe would *not* receive. Just a few decades after, a new and deadly conflict erupted. It was known as the Crimean War, and would last from 1853 to 1856, pitting the sons and grandsons of those veterans of the Napoleonic Wars in another war of the major global powers.

The Crimean War was the largest armed conflict of the European major powers since the time of Bonaparte. Less than forty years after Napoleon's crushing defeat at Waterloo, the world's greatest players once more rose up in arms, again painting the pages of history in bold hues of blood-red. This war was brief but vicious. Waged at the halfway mark of the 19th century, it is considered by many as the first true "modern" war. This becomes especially true once we consider the fact that the war pioneered numerous new strategies and tactics, new and modernized weaponry, and military technologies. What is more, the hard lessons learned in the Crimean War spurred the development and further exploration of complex military research.

Why was it so hard for the powers at hand to find common grounds, even after warring bitterly against one another during the Napoleonic Wars? Why did they resort to the same old practices of pitting young men in gruelling line battles for causes superficial at best? And more importantly, were there greater underlying causes to the Crimean War, things that were not resolved those four decades preceding? In this book we will attempt to answer those questions, to take a deeper look into this bitter and confusing war as we try to bring justice to the men that perished in it.

A Confusion of Causes: The Background of the Crimean War

In many ways, the Crimean War was a continuation of the Napoleonic Wars, a way for unsettled matters to be finally resolved. During the period of the 19th century, one of the major political issues that threatened the peace and stability in Europe was the so-called *"Eastern question"*, and the *"Sick man of the Bosphorus"*. This nickname referred to the Ottoman Empire, and the continuity and slow decay of this relic of the Middle Ages that struggled to survive in the increasingly modern times. The main opponent of the Ottoman Empire was, of course, Russia, that slumbering giant of the east that was one of the principal enemies of Napoleon in the previous war. Russia had centuries-old tendencies of getting an exit to the Mediterranean Sea, and the main way to achieve this goal was through the Ottoman territories. To that end, Russia waged an incredible *ten* wars with the Ottomans from 1568 until 1829, and their goal was not fully achieved. This continued conflict was a crucial threat to the stability and balance between the leading European powers.

But as the Ottoman Empire, that "sick man of Europe", was now truly sick and frail, the Russians were determined to destroy it and gain control of the Dardanelles and the Bosphorus, two major assets that would grant it an entrance to the Mediterranean. Of course, such tendencies and aspirations were not unobserved. Europe's greatest powers all had a say in the matter, as alliances, borders, and the power balance would all be threatened if the borders of Russia were to change. France and Britain were the foremost to oppose this: if Russia was to gain entry to the Mediterranean Sea, the fragile power balance that was carefully maintained ever since the Vienna Congress of 1815 would be entirely disturbed. More precisely, the shifting of the borders would have a direct impact on the British naval routes towards India and the Far East, and on the French interests in Turkey.

The Russian *tsar* (Emperor) Nicholas I, kept constant diplomatic pressures on the Ottoman Empire, in hopes to achieve his goals. He also aimed to gain the support of the Austrian Empire and Great Britain through diplomatic negotiations, but found nothing more than negative answers and spite from all European powers. This is due to the simple fact that the "Western Allies", i.e. Austria, Britain, and France chiefly, all saw the ambitions of Nicholas I as expansionists and as a direct threat to their own aspirations. But the goals of Nicholas and the Russians were not *just* political or strategic – they were also religious. A constant point of contention that threatened to grow out of proportions was *religion*. With the Russians being Eastern Orthodox Christians, and the Ottoman Turks being Muslims, common ground was nearly impossible to achieve. To make matters worse, Nicholas I had to take a defensive stance to aid the oppressed Christians within the Ottoman Empire who were treated as second-class citizens and were obliged to pay special taxes. To that end, Nicholas demanded that Orthodox Christians within the Ottoman Empire were to be placed under his protection. Further conflict erupted over the old question of Palestine and Jerusalem, with the question of control of the Holy Sepulcher. At the time, this holy Christian site was within the Ottoman Empire.

A brand new and turning tide within these tensions appeared with the rise of Napoleon III, who was proclaimed the Emperor of the French in 1852. This new ruler at France's helm had great aspirations and sought to restore the French grandeur of preceding decades. He saw the ongoing tensions and conflicts between the Ottomans and Russia as a way to confirm his legitimacy and prestige, and was thus quick to enter into it. To that end, Napoleon III quickly took a stance in defense of the French interests and the Catholic minorities within Jerusalem.

PEACE WON BY THE SABER: THE CRIMEAN WAR, 1853-18565

This was directly opposed to the Russian interests and Nicholas I, who stood in defense of the Eastern Orthodox Christians, to whom he felt obliged to help. In many ways, the Russians felt misunderstood. Many historians consider their foreign policy to have been entirely wrong and mismanaged, and that their intentions towards the Ottoman have been understood incorrectly. At the time of the Crimean War, Nicholas I himself – as did the other Russians – believed that his intentions to protect the Christian minorities was taken completely wrongly. This surviving snippet from a letter shows us the perfect insight into the way Russians were perceived at the time, being (somewhat) falsely accused of having expansionist ambitions.

"France takes Algeria from Turkey, and almost every year England annexes another Indian principality: none of this disturbs the balance of power; but when Russia occupies Moldavia and Wallachia, albeit only temporarily, that disturbs the balance of power. France occupies Rome and stays there several years during peacetime: that is nothing; but Russia only thinks of occupying Constantinople, and the peace of Europe is threatened. The English declare war on the Chinese (First Opium War), who have, it seems, offended them: no one has the right to intervene; but Russia is obliged to ask Europe for permission if it quarrels with its neighbor. England threatens Greece to support the false claims of a miserable Jew and burns its fleet: that is a lawful action; but Russia demands a treaty to protect millions of Christians, and that is deemed to strengthen its position in the East at the expense of the balance of power. We can expect nothing from the West but blind hatred and malice..."

— Mikhail Pogodin's memorandum to Nicholas I, 1853

The Russian Tsar issued an ultimatum to the Ottoman Sultan in 1853, demanding that a Russian protectorate be given to the 12 million Christian subjects within the Ottoman Empire itself. Meanwhile, the French and the British entered into a strong alliance in order to defend their mutual interests within the Mediterranean chiefly, and have essentially stood in the defense of the Ottoman Empire. That same year they have bolstered the hopes of the Ottoman Sultan, who at once refused the Russian Ultimatum. And with all the diplomatic attempts to settle the disputes and the unstable situation, a war was almost inevitable.

In July of 1853, the Russian emperor Nicholas I responded to his rejected ultimatum by ordering two of his imperial armies in Bessarabia, 80,000 men strong, to occupy the Danubian Principalities of Moldavia and Wallachia, thus invading Ottoman territories by crossing the Prut river. In response, the Ottoman Empire – encouraged by the support of the British and the French – declared war on the Russians in October of 1853. Thus the Crimean War officially began.

A Sudden Outbreak: The Early Stages of the War

The occupation of Wallachia and Moldavia was in many ways the first logical step of Nicholas I. These two regions, traditionally Christian, were directly to the south of Russia's borders within Eastern Europe proper. The two Russian armies under the command of general Gorchakov numbered roughly 80,000 men. Their first stop after crossing the Prut River was the occupation of the town of Jassy. Furthermore, the Russian consul in Bucharest demanded that the principalities of Wallachia and Moldavia both cease with the payment of taxes to the Porte (the Ottoman center), and that they cease any further relations with it as well. The similar demand was made from the Serbian *knyaz*, Aleksandar Karađorđević (1842-1885). Interestingly, both representatives of Wallachia and Moldavia refused this demand, as did the Serbian knyaz. They all sought neutrality in the conflict, and thus remained "loyal" to the Ottoman Porte. Still, the Russian demand for the cessation of tax payment was a clear indication of the actual Russian intentions: to assert full control of the Danubian Principalities and for good, despite the reassurances of Nicholas I that the occupation was only temporary.

Needless to say, the major European powers quickly reacted to this activity of the Russians. The Austrian Empire, whose southeastern borders were adjacent to both Russia and the Danubian Principalities, reacted by mobilizing some 25,000 soldiers on its southern borders. In many ways, this was a show of force, a way to threaten the oppressed Slavic peoples both in its own lands and in Serbia that they should remain neutral and not to side with the Russians, their traditional kinsmen and allies. The French and the British also reacted. Their powerful naval fleets were already sent as a precaution to the Dardanelles. Now, as a reaction to Russian invasion, they were placed under alert and were ready to act, sitting moored in the Dardanelles' Besika Bay.

And although the war was not yet begun as Europe observed Russian actions, the Ottomans also reacted to the incursion into their lands. The Porte ordered the famed Rumelian Omar Pasha Latas to begin strengthening the numerous fortresses along the Danube river, and to prepare for the defense of the realm. Furthermore, the Ottomans sought reinforcements from their southern regions, notably the Pashaliks of Tunisia and Egypt. From the latter, Abbas Pasha sent roughly 22,000 men, while the Tunisian Pasha sent some 7,000 men, 12 cannons, and 700 horses.

Even with this major intrusion, which could have easily been dubbed as an invasion, neither side immediately went to war. The Ottoman Sultan could have used this invasion as a *"casus belli"* (cause of war), but staved off his decision. The Russian Emperor, on the other hand, claimed that his military activity was only temporary, and served as a pressure on the Sultan, all with the aim of furthering Nicholas' goal of protecting Orthodox Christians within the Ottoman Empire. The Ottoman Porte issued an official protest note against the Russian occupation of its principalities on July 15th, after which a series of intense diplomatic negotiations followed, and all in order to avoid warfare.

Alas, the growing tensions between Russia and Turkey were all clear indications of a looming conflict. Russia's apparent expansionism, masked by their alleged struggle for Christian minority rights, was a major thorn in the sides of the Western European powers, who were quick to stand behind the Ottomans in defense.

The British ambassador to the Ottoman Empire, Stratford Canning, 1st Viscount Stratford de Redcliffe, was one of the crucial figures in the developments preceding the outbreak of war. Based in Constantinople (modern Istanbul), Stratford found himself in the midst of the ongoing crisis, which was then seen as the dispute between chiefly Napoleon III and Nicholas I, over the protection of the holy Christian places in Jerusalem chiefly. Stratford was the first to receive the news of the Russian demands to the counts of Wallachia and Moldavia, and was thus keen to ask for a determined military action. In recent times, Stratford is accused of *"encouraging the Turks to reject the compromise agreement"*, consistently indicating to the Ottomans that any treaty proposed by the Russians would ultimately lead to the Ottoman Empire being reduced to a protectorate under the Russian Emperor Nicholas I.

However, the dispute over the rights of Christians within the Ottoman Empire was only the superficial cause of conflict, a mask beneath which lay deeper and more serious aims of expansion and power. The European allied powers were well aware that they could not allow the Russians to dissect the ailing Ottoman Empire and thus expand its borders towards the Mediterranean. To that end, Great Britain, France, Austria, and Prussia, agreed to act together in order in a peace initiative. Austria was equally affected by the threat of Russian expansion, since their foreign trade directly depended on the Danube river waterways. Thus, it could not tolerate the Russian occupation of the Danubian Principalities of Wallachia and Moldavia. For that reason, Austria took on the role of leading a diplomatic peace process that involved chiefly the exchange of diplomatic notes between the major European capitals, which was further exacerbated due to the lack of telegraph connections between Constantinople (Istanbul) and the other European metropolises. Prussia was also a part of that alliance since it generally followed Austrian leadership.

The Last Failed Attempts at Peace

The peace initiative taken by the allies was centered on mediating the growing conflict between the Russians and the Ottomans. The culmination of these diplomatic activities is the so-called "Vienna Note" of 1853. Many considered that the diplomacy of Emperor Nicholas I had taken Russia to the brink of war, despite no initial intentions of creating a forced conflict. Fearing the consequences of such a war, the Great Powers agreed to the aforementioned Vienna Note of August 1853. However, the Porte subsequently refused to accept the mediation of the Great Powers, and declared war on Russia in October 1853. The Vienna Note was a document put together at a special conference in Vienna, created chiefly by the Austrian Foreign Minister, count Karl Ferdinand von Buol, together with the British and French ministers, and all in the name of the Ottoman Empire.

The "note" was a diplomatic document that was created solely with the purpose to stave off war and end hostilities, and the contents of the document were purposefully written with a subtle pro-Russian tone. The tone likely stemmed from the increasingly tenuous position that Austria found itself in.

It's Foreign Minister, Count Buol, had a difficult task mediating between Britain and France on one side, and Russia on the other. This is due to the fact that the Russian Emperor Nicholas expected a good deal of assistance from Austria, hoping to have them as allies in the matter. Most notably, this was due Russia's assistance in Austrian matters in the decades before. Nicholas I intervened on Austria's behalf to help suppress the Hungarian Revolt of 1848, and later intervened again on its behalf to help against Prussia and create the Agreement at Olmütz in 1850. To that matter, Austrians were somewhat "in debt" to the Russians, and Nicholas relied on the fact. Another fact that made matters more difficult for the Austrians was their geographic position. If war was to erupt, pitting France and Britain against Russia, it was obvious that Austria would bear the brunt of the fighting, sharing borders with both sides. To that end, Count Buol struggled to find the balanced middle ground, thus mediating between the involved parties.

Luckily, on July 31st 1853, France and Britain agreed to the terms specified by the Vienna Note. It's contents, carefully devised by Buol, dictated that a "joint Russo-Turkish concern for the well-being of the Orthodox Christians in the Ottoman Empire" would be established. It also stated that the Ottoman Sultan would respect the former treaties of *Küçük Kaynarca (1774)* and of *Adrianople (1829)*, that he will ensure that the Greeks were to share in the advantages awarded to the Orthodox Christians, and a reaffirmation to *"maintain the status quo in the Holy Land and to not disturb this status quo without combined consent of France and Russia"*. Finally, the note guaranteed the Russian right to build a church and hospice in the holy city of Jerusalem.

The Russian Emperor was pleased with the solution and considered the Vienna Note a diplomatic victory. Their acceptance of the note was expected, particularly to its pro-Russian tone, and on August 3rd, the Russians accepted the terms. However, trouble soon followed, this time from the Ottoman side. On 19th of August, the Ottoman Porte amended the note, declining to sign it. They issued a protest, claiming that the interference of the Russians and the French – particularly in the third point of the note – was a direct infringement on Turkish sovereignty. Furthermore, the Porte objected to the "audacity" of the European great power to take it upon themselves and draw a note *"without the knowledge of the party more immediately involved"*. They officially rejected the Vienna Note on September 20th, 1853.

The Ottomans believed that the note would give Russia the right to meddle in Ottoman affairs, and thus requested the revisions. Their claims proved to be substantiated, particularly after the publishing of a private diplomatic document in a Berlin newspaper that stated that the Russians, through the note, had the right to intervene for the protection of Orthodox Christians on the *entire* territory of the Ottoman Empire – and not just in the areas of Jerusalem. To that end, the Porte demanded that the Vienna Note was to be accepted only with the added changes that they provided, which accentuated the sovereignty of the Ottoman Empire, and their rights and privileges over the Orthodox Christians according to the Sultan's will, and not according to the Russian demands or peace treaties.

The Russians rejected these changes outright, which activated a multitude of military implications. The outbreak of war became imminent, as the diplomatic mediation failed completely. The French and British sent further fleets towards Istanbul, as a way to protect the Sultan. On the other hand, the Russian troops based in the Danubian Principalities remained there, and vowed to stay until a peaceful solution was found. In response to this continued military presence in its territories, the Ottoman Empire declared war on Russia on October 4th 1853. The great chess-board of war was now fully set-up: the British and the French found themselves too invested in the Ottoman interests, and it was too late to withdraw from the looming conflict. A large-scale war was about to be unleashed.

In the meantime, just before the declaration of war, certain events transpired within the Ottoman Empire itself. A part of the core Ottoman populace, centered on Istanbul, displayed a new enthusiasm for a fight, likely instigated by the *ulema*, the religious scholarly elite within Islam. A new wave of religious zealotry appeared: the students of the *madrasas* (*"any type of educational institution, secular or religious, whether for elementary instruction or higher learning"*) organized demonstrations in favor of a war against the "infidels". Furthermore, numerous posters began appearing, displayed chiefly on the doors of the *padishah's* mosque, calling for a "holy war". Next were the students of the religious schools, who were increasingly displeased with the latest regulations of the *"tanzimat"*, the period of reform within the Empire that began in 1839. This tanzimat began promoting secular schools, which further affected the wave of discontent and the demonstration that called for a holy war. All of these issues made for a very real threat of a revolution against the government – if the latter would refuse to declare war upon Russia. To that end there followed an increased pressure from the thirty-four religious leaders within the

Ottoman Empire on the Porte itself. On 12th September, these leaders held a meeting with the Sultan, where they gave him an ultimatum: either he declares war on Russia, or abdicates from the throne. That very same evening, the Sultan made arrangements with his ministers to declare war, but not until the Porte would acquire the guarantees of support from the Western European allies, and not until the religious demonstrations in Istanbul were placed under control.

These demonstrations alarmed the European consuls within Istanbul: there was a widespread fear of fanatic reprisals and a massacre of minority Christians within the Empire. The French official, Edmond de la Cour, alarmed the British Secretary of State for Foreign Affairs, Lord Clarendon, who in turn arranged the dispatch of the British naval fleet to Istanbul on 23rd September, as added help for the quelling of the revolution.

So, we can see that the public atmosphere "at home" for the Ottomans was quite focused on warfare, even though many domestic and foreign military commanders expressed their doubts in the capabilities of the Ottoman forces in a war against Russia. And even so, the religious leaders continued to insist on war, and were even bolstered by Mustafa

Reşid Pasha, who even exclaimed that *"it is better to die with arms in hand than to die with tied hands. Inshallah (God willing), we will be victorious and destroy the harmful treaties as well!"*

Thus, when the Ottoman declaration of war finally arrived in October, it was welcomed by the general public. It was published in the official newspapers, the *"Takvim-i Vekayi"* on October 4th 1853, after which followed the declaration of the Ottoman manifesto, with which the government justified its declaration of war through the refusal of the Russians to withdraw its armies from the occupied Danubian principalities.

And thus, the stage for war was set. Today, some one hundred and sixty nine years later, historians continue to study the exact causes of this conflict. Many have called the Crimean War a truly confusing conflict, a war whose causes have shown an enormous *"confusion of purpose"*, which inadvertently led to a vicious war, famously dubbed as *"notoriously incompetent international butchery"*. When studied in depth, the causes of the war can be "pinned" to any of the belligerent parties. In fact, it is quite easy to become biased when observing the causes: as historians did over the decades following the war. Every ruler had his own cause to "stand his ground" and ultimately lead his nation to war. Whether it was necessary or not, is a different question altogether. The British historian, Alan Taylor, writes that *"the Crimean war was fought for the sake of Europe rather than for the Eastern question; it was fought against Russia, not in favor of Turkey... The British fought Russia out of resentment and supposed that her defeat would strengthen the European Balance of Power."*

Many have said that the defense of the Ottoman Empire was simply a pretense, a necessary excuse that the Western Allies needed in order to solidify their prestige and to save their own interests in the Mediterranean. On the other hand, the same can be said of Russia:

their intentions can be easily seen as expansionist, as their Emperor greedily swooped in on the frail and aging rival of Russia, the Ottoman Empire.

"In some sense the Crimean war was predestined and had deep-seated causes." Alan Taylor writes in his 1954 masterwork, "The Struggle for Mastery in Europe 1848–1918". *"Neither Nicholas I nor Napoleon III nor the British government could retreat in the conflict for prestige once it was launched. Nicholas needed a subservient Turkey for the sake of Russian security; Napoleon needed success for the sake of his domestic position; the British government needed an independent Turkey for the security of the Eastern Mediterranean... Mutual fear, not mutual aggression, caused the Crimean war."*

On the other hand, many one-sided or biased looks were made on the causes of the war. For example, Baron Alexandre Jomini, a member of the Russian Foreign Office, presents in his study the views of Prince Alexander Mikhailovich Gorchakov, the Russian Foreign Minister from 1856 to 1882, attempting to unfold the events that led to the war. Jomini states that it was the French foreign policy that created the Holy Places crisis in the first place. He also writes that the combined Ottoman, French, and British actions had forced Russia into an "unwanted conflict". He claims that Emperor Nicholas I only wanted to maintain the status quo within the Ottoman Empire, and to defend the interests of Russia concerning the Russian Orthodox minority. The one-sidedness of this study can be quickly observed through its pro-Russian stance.

Others, like the British author Alexander William Kinglake, describe the outbreak of the war as the direct outcome of Napoleon III's foreign policy after 1850. In his major study of the war, published in 1863, Mr. Kinglake presents the theory that Napoleon III pursued a quite aggressive foreign policy in the eastern Mediterranean, hoping to solidify his own position at home and to shift the attention of the French people away from domestic issues to those abroad. According to Kinglake, Napoleon III's actions created a conflict with Russia over the Holy Places, and subsequently drew in Britain into the conflict in order to protect French interests.

Alas, in the end, it mattered little at whom the finger of blame was to land. Each major power had its own causes and desires to enter into the fray. For Russia it was the expansion of its border towards the Mediterranean and the final square-off with its centuries-old rival, the Ottoman Empire. For the latter, it was mere survival, and the buckling of its Sultan under the pressures of the Islamic populace that was thirsty for a holy war. For France, it was a chance to solidify the influence of the newly appointed Napoleon III – and the protection of its foreign interests. For Britain, it was the securing of its trade abroad, and the protection of its maritime routes. And for Austria and Prussia it was the matter of delicate diplomacy, the protection of its borders, and the mounting pressures of the Western allies. In the end, a lot of it had to do with *prestige*. As the bickering and rivalry threatened to turn into all out warfare, the leaders found themselves too invested to back out. It was a matter of saving face and committing to the cause. Even if the price of it was millions of human lives.

The First Conflicts – Clashes on the Danubian Front

In the days before the actual declaration of war, there was a lot of commotion between the rival powers. As the deafening crescendo of impending war was reaching its culminating point, some final attempts at staving off the inevitable were made. As a sign of "peaceful intentions", the chief commander of the Ottoman Rumelian troops, Omar Pasha Latas, announced to the Russian general that he would allow 15 days for their troops to evacuate the Danubian principalities – before he would proceed to attack. In many ways, this was a bluff: the Ottomans were actually quite unprepared to wage another war with Russia, and this 15-day "ultimatum" was actually their way of buying more time to pressure the western allies to help, and to quell the rebellious currents within Istanbul.

On October 10th, the Russian General Gorchakov responded to Omer Pasha Latas' ultimatum by saying how he has no jurisdiction to withdraw his armies. Legally seen, this was the true date of the total declaration of war between the two powers. After the 15-day ultimatum expired, the Ottomans began their attack on the occupied Danubian Principalities – contrary to the advice of the western allies. The Ottomans did so while counting on the help of the western media, as they allocated great funds to promote their cause in the papers abroad. In the autumn of 1853, the Ottoman government greatly funded its embassy in London, creating public demonstrations and publishing newspaper articles, both of which called the British government to act against Russia. In the meantime, the Ottoman commander Reshid Pasha feared that the Russians would orchestrate a surprise attack on Istanbul, and to that end he asked the British and the French for help. The two powers agreed to assist, and relocated their naval fleets from the Dardanelles to Istanbul, thus protecting the

Sultan. And following the Ottoman declaration of war, the Russians officially declared war as well, through an Emperor's memorandum published on November 1st 1853.

With the war officially started, the world waited for the first move – as if on a grand chess board. It was generally expected that the Ottoman Empire was to make the first move, considering that it was their territory under occupation. And so it was that on October 21st 1853, at the mouth of the Danube, near the Isakchi (İsakçı) fortress, the first hostilities erupted between Russia and the Ottomans. Here, the Ottoman shore batteries opened fire upon two Russian steamships that were headed towards Galatz. However, although this can be considered as the first actual conflict of the war, it was only a minor skirmish, and everyone waited for an actual large confrontation.

What about the armies directly involved within the disputed Danubian Principalities? What where the positions and the numbers deployed in the first steps of the Crimean War? The Ottoman Empire relied on their Rumelian army here. It was commanded by the seasoned general *Müşir Ömer Pasha,* the man who was chiefly responsible for quelling revolts in Arabia, Kurdistan, and Bosnia, and a commander full of zeal and at the height of his military career. A man fluent in several modern languages, Müşir Ömer Pasha was considered the finest Ottoman commander by both the French and the British. Others, however, did not share this view. The Russian military reports that were compiled before the outbreak of war were not so quick to shower this commander with compliments. In fact, they doubted his abilities. What is more, the French commander-in-chief, Marshal Saint-Arnaud – the man whose opinion was valued – stated that Müşir Ömer Pasha is a good general, but one needing guidance. Furthermore, Saint-Arnaud commented on the Ottoman army itself, noticing how it had a high command, and soldiers aplenty – but no officers and few NCO's. Many saw this as a critical flaw. To make matters even worse, the high command of the Rumelian Army was not ideal. The chief of staff (and later deputy) of Müşir Ömer Pasha's Rumelian army was one Ferik Çerkez İsmail Pasha. Another chief of staff was Nazir Ahmed Pasha. The issue at hand was that these two men did not like each other at all. Furthermore, Ömer Pasha saw Ferik Pasha as a direct rival, and to that end tried to undermine him wherever possible. This discontent amongst the highest commanders was not an ideal circumstance, and would even have effect in some subsequent battles.

Nevertheless, the Rumelian army was considered the best Ottoman army when considering their provisions, officers, arms, training, and discipline. In fact, its supplies of arms and provisions were not at all infernal when compared to the Russian ones. In summary, the number of men that the Rumelian army had against the Russians was roughly from 145 to 178 thousand men. This massive force was spread out along the Danube River, in the many fortresses and cities that stretched from Vidin to Varna. These included Rusçuk, Silistria, Kalafat, Varna, Vidin, Tutrakan, Zіştovi, and Şumnu.

Opposing this vast army was the seasoned Russian commander, Field Marshal Ivan Fyodorovich Paskevich, the famed Count of Erevan and Prince of Warsaw. This veteran leader was noted for his exploits against the Persians from 1826 to 1828, at Erzurum from 1828 to 1829, in Warsaw in 1831, and during the Hungarian Revolution from 1848 to 1849. Through his prestige and veterancy, Paskevich was a much respected commander, held in high esteem by the Russian Emperor Nicholas I who affectionately called him "father-commander" ("otets-komandir"). However, Paksevich was 72 at the time and lost his early zeal and initiative. What is more, he openly opposed the Crimean War – an opinion that he could not express publicly. Well aware that this was likely the final campaign in his career, Paskevich was too hesitant and careful in the initial stages of the war. He was afraid of staining his remarkable reputation by suffering an early defeat on the Danube, and thus acted too cautiously, with much hesitation. It was later stated that this hesitation had a negative impact on Russian efforts on the Danube. But even so, Paskevich had a high opinion of the Russian troops, noting that the Ottomans were not an equal match. On 23rd of September 1853, he writes to Emperor Nicholas:

"As is known, the Turks are strong in fortresses, but they cannot hold out against our troops on the field. It is necessary to maneuver in such a way as to lure them out of their fortresses and smash them... I do not share the idea that the Turks could dream of causing us great damage from the Asian side. The Turkish cavalry, the Kurds, have always been beaten by our Muslims and our line troops... As regards their regular troops, they are not frightening in Europe, and even less in Asia."

Paskevich held command of roughly 88,000 soldiers present in Wallachia and Moldavia, with headquarters in Bucharest. However, he was not to hold this command for too long. He was wounded on June 9th 1854 and prompted to return to Russia due to his advanced age. He was replaced as the commander of the army by his chief of staff, Mikhail Dmitrevich Gorchakov, a general that was not known for his initiative and resolution, but rather for his obeying of orders.

The Ottoman Commander Omer Pasha Latas concentrated a considerable force around the fortress of Vidin, the westernmost fortress on the Danube. This fort had great strategic importance, and the Russians were well aware of that fact. However, they did not position troops here due to the proximity of the Serbian borders. If they had done so, they risked antagonizing the Austrians – a thing they did not need. Even commander Paskevich, as part of his caution and hesitation, noted his fear of Austrians entering on Ottoman side, possibly threatening to crush his armies in a pincer movement.

The first engagement of the war quickly followed, when Omer Pasha Latas crossed Danube at Vidin, joined his forces with citizens of adjacent Calafat region, and quickly conquered the Cossack city of Calafat. At the very same time, on the eastern side, Ottomans crossed the Danube at Silistra, advancing towards the city of Oltenița, where they engaged the Russians. This led to the very first major battle of the Crimean War, the *Battle of Oltenița* of November 4th, 1853. At Oltenița, the Russian General Dannenberg faced the fortified line positions of the Ottomans under Omer Pasha. Attempting to weaken Ottoman positions with artillery, Dannenberg marched his men in thick line columns, suffering heavy losses and sounding retreat at the last moment. The battle – although indecisive – was a tactical victory for the Ottomans, who won their first major engagement in the war. And although it was not a major battle per se – with only a few hundred casualties – it was a boost for the Ottoman moral. The leading European papers quickly reported of the "great Turkish triumph" at Oltenița, much to the shame of the Russians.

This first major clash of the war was a wake-up call for the Russians. The Russian Emperor aimed at a major offensive against the Ottomans, but his views were not shared by commander Ivan Paskevich. The latter considered that the Ottomans were too strong – in numbers especially – and that the fleets of the western allies were too close for comfort. He instead proposed that the Russian armies ought to be fortified at defensive positions on the northern side of the Danube, and that Christian militias should be organized south of the river. He considered that the Russian influence amongst the Christian and Slavic minorities within the Ottoman Empire was the most powerful of all Russian "weapons". Ivan Paskevich was also well aware of the Austrian threat. If they were to attack, everything could easily crumble to pieces. For this reason, Paskevich concentrated on consolidating his positions along the Danube, relying on the river as the supply line for his troops.

To Emperor Nicholas he writes that he hopes of closer ties with the Serbs, Herzegovinians, Montenegrins, and Bulgarians - Slavs and Orthodox Christians that could crush the Turks with Russian help.

The Ottomans on the other hand, fearing of losing their Balkan territories that were occupied by Slavs who were majority Christians, decided to maintain the defensive line on the Danube and to shift focus on the Caucasus. They planned to attack there, knowing that the Russians began lowering the number of their troops there, sending them instead towards the Danube front. They also had a similar view as the Russians: they hoped to utilize the added help of the Muslim tribes that dwelt alongside the coasts of the Black Sea, just as the Russians hoped for the assistance of Slavic minorities in the Balkans. With enough troops and the mobilizing of Islamic tribes, the Ottomans hoped to entirely crush Russian rule within the Caucasus region. Furthermore, they counted on the support of the British, who were – over a period of several years – secretly supplying Georgian and Circassian rebels with both money and weapons. And even though the Ottomans have officially stepped down from all aspirations towards the Caucasus in the Treaty of Adrianople of 1829, the eruption of the Crimean War changed the circumstances, once again opening the way towards the coveted region. To that end, on October 9th, the Ottoman Sultan called the religious leader of the Islamic tribes of northern Caucasus, Imam Shamil, to rise up in a holy war and to defend Islam against the Russians in the Caucasus. Imam Shamil was to work together with the Anatolian Ottoman armies, commanded by Abdi Pasha.

Already after some 20 days, the first assaults in the Caucasus occurred. The Russian fortress of Saint Nicholas in Batumi (modern-day Georgia), fell under the assaults of Abdi Pasha's volunteer cavalry and *bashi-bazouks*, irregular troops infamous for their brutality and disorderly behavior. The Bashi-bazouks were ruthless and often resorted to massacres and genocides. In the mid 1800s, such conduct was considered highly controversial, and would become the subject of much debate in western society. Reports from Batumi only added to the controversy: the Ottoman bashi-bazouks tortured, raped, and massacred hundreds of civilians (largely Christians), and killed several thousands of Cossack troops. Furthermore, a ship full of Georgian children was sold into slavery in Istanbul. These crimes – by that time belonging in the Middle Ages – completely alienated the Georgian people – both Muslims and Christians – against the Ottoman Empire. On the Advice of the Western allies, in hopes of winning back the sympathies of the Georgians, the Ottomans returned the enslaved children, but to no avail. They have completely lost the trust of the Georgians, who from that point on became the most steadfast Russian allies.

A Disaster for the Ottoman Fleet: The Battle of Sinop, November 1853

The Ottoman land offensives in the Caucasus were very much dependent on the supplies from their Black Sea fleets. However, the Ottoman naval power was still in the process of recovery, especially since suffering a devastating defeat at the Battle of Navarino in 1827, where 60 of their ships had sunk to the bottom of the Ionian Sea. However, they now had the added support of the French and British naval fleet with some five ships of the line and another thirty support vessels. They also had at their disposal the Egyptian fleet that numbered some 10 war ships under the command of Halil Pasha. With all these forces combined, the Ottoman navy was just enough to stand against the Russian naval power, and to keep them hesitant from committing to any large scale operations on the waters. But the Russians knew very well that the Ottoman fleet was their pulsating lifeline that supplied their troops in the Caucasus. To that end, the Russian commander-in-chief on land and sea, Prince Alexander Menshikov, ordered admiral Vladimir Kornilov and vice-admiral Pavel Nakhimov (who were patrolling the western and eastern Black Sea respectively) to destroy all and any Ottoman ships carrying supplies to the Caucasus. The Ottomans, on the other hand, were well aware of these Russian patrols, and thus decided to send a smaller fleet into the Black Sea, hoping that the English and the French would rush to help in case of a Russian attack.

In late 1853, the Ottoman fleet was split into four separate squadrons. Ahmed Pasha was tasked with protecting the Ottoman, Allied, and neutral trade vessels; the Egyptian commander Hasan Pasha was tasked with transporting soldiers to Varna and patrolling the Rumelian coasts; Mustafa Pasha was tasked with servicing the coasts of Georgia, Anatolia, and Circassia; while the fourth squadron, commanded by

Osman Pasha, had the task of patrolling northwestern Anatolian coasts, from Amasra to Sinop. The Ottomans caught wind of the Russian patrols close to northern Anatolia, roughly 200 kilometers away from Istanbul, and thus sent the squadron of Osman Pasha to perform reconnaissance. However, the latter was troubled by strong storm winds, and had to anchor at the port of Sinop. The Ottoman admiral Mustafa Pasha quickly recognized the unfavorable position of the anchored fleet, and at once departed for Istanbul to warn of the threat. And soon after, the news of a Russian squadron near Sinop were received. On November 30th, the Ottomans sent word to the British and the French, asking help, but the two powers jointly agreed that it was not recommended to dispatch their fleets to the Black Sea at that moment.

The notable Russian commander, Pavel Nakhimov, descended upon the fleet anchored at Sinop in the early morning hours of November 30th, 1853. His force consisted of just 6 ships of the line, 2 frigates, and 3 steamers, while the Ottomans relied on 7 frigates, 3 corvettes, and 2 steamers. With accurate fire from the cannons of his squadron, Nakhimov utterly ravaged the anchored Ottoman fleet. The Russian's adopted special explosive shells for their naval artillery just sometime prior to the war: the Battle of Sinop was the very first time these shells were used in combat. And they proved to be a revolutionary new weapon – the high explosive shelling decimated the wooden vessels and caused heavy losses. These shells would penetrate the wooden construction of a ship and only then release their explosive charge with devastating effects.

In a short time, all the Ottoman ships were destroyed and were beyond repair. Just one steamship managed to flee the carnage, even before the onslaught began. Curiously, this sole surviving ship carried the British Admiral Adolphus Slade onboard, the naval advisor to the Turks. The man relied on the speed of his steamship to flee before the advancing Russians.

The attack of Pavel Nakhimov was intense. Even after all the Ottoman ships were sunk and blown to smithereens, the Russian fleet continued to rain high explosive shells upon the port city of Sinop and the coastal batteries it had. Much of the town was blown up or set ablaze, in particular the city quarters with Muslim citizens. The battle was largely one-sided: the Russians lost no ships, with only a few vessels suffering minor damage. They also lost 37 men in the fighting, and had 229 wounded. In comparison, the Ottomans lost all their ships (but one), and around 3,000 of their men were killed. The coastal batteries and parts of the city of Sinop were also devastated, and around 150 men were captured, including the leader, naval officer Osman Pasha.

At home in Russia, the news of the victory at Sinop caused a flurry of joyous emotions. Celebrations were held, and the Russian Navy finally proved itself as capable and powerful. But what is more important, this battle was a pioneering one in many regards, and it served as an all-important step-stone that would totally change naval warfare practices. The foremost change was the first-time use of explosive shells and the Paixhans cannons that fired them. The shells had both kinetic and explosive damage, and were extremely devastating against wood-clad ships of the line. At Sinop, their combat use and effectiveness were proven: the Ottoman vessels stood no chance. This new military technology would cause quite a stir, and would change the concepts of naval artillery for centuries to follow. The age of wooden ships was obviously coming to an end. The French ruler Napoleon III at once ordered the ships of the French fleet to be ironclad, as a means of increased protection.

The Ottomans suffered a terrible defeat in the first major naval battle of the war. The defeat renewed the diplomatic negotiations, and already by 5th December, the Austrian minister of foreign affairs, count Buol, presented a new list of peace conditions at a conference in Vienna. These were peace conditions of the Ottoman Porte, orchestrated together with Austria, Prussia, Britain, and France. The conditions still demanded that the Russians were to leave the occupied Danubian Principalities of Wallachia and Moldavia, but were also offering the renewing of the previous treaties with Russia and the acceptance of their conditions and demands in relation to the Holy Places dispute. When the Ottoman Porte accepted these new conditions presented in Vienna, Istanbul once again erupted in open revolt. New student demonstrations flared across the capital, and increased rumors of a massacre of the town's Christians began circulating. Reshid Pasha, the chief Ottoman statesman who was responsible for the Tanzimat reforms, quickly resigned from his position, fearing for his own safety at home. The Istanbul demonstrations were quelled only when around 160 students were arrested and deported to Crete. But even so, it was clear that peace was now a lost opportunity: blood was shed, and the people wanted satisfaction of justice. The vicious Battle of Sinop deeply shook the balance of European powers. Many however, doubted the one-sidedness of the clash, painting it rather as an ambush or something even worse. But no matter what, the battle was a legitimate act under the rules of war: which by that point was already declared on both sides. Yet even so, the British propaganda machine dubbed this clash a massacre, citing excessive bombardment of the town and many civilian victims. With these allegations, the British wanted to incite the public to further dislike the Russians, and even went so far as to petition Queen Victoria, demanding a more "active attitude" on her part.

On the other hand, the French leader, Napoleon III, used this opportunity to strengthen his alliance with the British, and to further distract the view of the public from his domestic issues, to those abroad. He also proposed to the British that the two of their fleets were to enter the Black Sea waters and thus force the Russians to return to their naval base at Sevastopol.

The Continued Danubian campaigns of 1854

In the spring, the war continued in its steady and ominous pace. The tensions at the Danubian principalities of Moldavia and Wallachia were now continuing, even after the Ottomans scored some initial first victories. The Russian emperor Nicholas I planned for a spring offensive, which meant that his armies were to cross the Danube River at Vidin and Silistra, besieging both cities, as well as the towns of Galatza and Brailovo. With that in place, the Russian troops – under the command of General Alexander Liders – marched between 23rd and 29th of March and took over the entire region of Dobruja, a major Ottoman province. The Russian plan was centered on the conquest of the fortress of Silistra, a powerful strongpoint that would give them some much needed foothold in the Danubian regions. It would allow them to use the Danube River as a supply route for their forces in the Black Sea, connecting the region with the Balkans. Their plan also considered dragging the Bulgarians into the conflict against the Ottomans, as the former were largely oppressed Christians that suffered immensely under the hands of Bashi-bazouks. Alas, the Russian advance was slow. The Ottomans offered stiff resistance on the northern side of the Danube. The Russian troops were further slowed because of a construction of a bridge across Danube near the place of Galai. They succeeded in crossing over, continuing southwards towards Silistra before getting stuck and slowed in the swampy grounds of Danube's delta, a sparsely populated and infertile area. Here, further difficulties abounded. With dwindling food supplies, disease and hunger quickly spread amongst the Russian troops. By April of 1854, of roughly 210,000 Russian troops, some 90,000 were out of action. One of the main sources of disease, besides the swampy grounds, was the bad food quality of the Russian soldier. Many surviving letters show us a crucial glimpse into the conditions "on the ground". These letters were sent by the common Russian soldiers, in which they asked their families for help through finances and food. Of course, all of these conditions further exacerbated the efforts of the Russian commander Ivan Paskevich. He was not only faced with the disease and slow progress of his troops: he now observed the accumulation of the Austrian forces on the borders with Serbia, with the closing-in of the British and French troops, and with the Ottomans who were fiercely guarding their fortified positions. All of these factors created a very much real threat of encirclement, a fact which Paskevich recognized at once. For this reason he continued to stave off the attack on Silistra, despite the mounting pressures of Emperor Nicholas I.

All the while, on 22nd April 1854, the naval fleets of the Western allies began their first all-out attack on Russian soil. This began with the bombardment of Odessa, an important Black Sea port. The allies caught news of massive supplies and troops massing at Odessa: some 60,000 soldiers and great amounts of ammunition, both intended for transport to the Danubian frontlines. But the truth was that Odessa was not at all full of supplies – it was lightly guarded with only a few artillery units and had modest military significance at the time. Nevertheless, the British sent an ultimatum to the governor of the city of Odessa, Dmitri Osten-Sacken. In it, they demanded the surrender of all ships anchored in the port. When no answer arrived, the united French and British fleet, commanded by Sir James Whitley Dundas, opened artillery fire upon Odessa. The ensuing devastation lasted for eleven hours straight, and caused incredible damage in the port, the destruction of its coastal batteries, the sinking of several ships, and the death of a dozen people. This one-sided affair, similar to the Battle of Sinop, was a clear announcement that the French and the British were closing in on the Danube theater of war. It was only a question of time when they were to rush to aid the Ottomans entrenched at Silistra and on the Danube. Furthermore, the bombardment effectively neutralized Odessa as a naval base, putting it "out of action" for the rest of the war and thus allowing the French and British fleets to freely roam the Black Sea, maintaining their supply lines.

The Battle of Silistra

In the meantime, the Russian Emperor continued the pressure upon his seasoned commander, Ivan Paskevich, regarding the siege of Silistra. The Russian high command was determined to penetrate within the Ottoman Balkan territories, and time was of the essence. To that end, Paskevich at last began a planned bombardment of Silistra in the middle of May 1854. However, the Ottomans used the time since the declaration of war to busily enhance the fortifications along the Danube, Silistra included. This was done under the watchful eye of colonel Grach, a Prussian military officer who was an expert on fortifications and mining. As a result, when the actual siege of the fortress began, the Ottomans resisted with a lot of resilience and ferocity. The actual battle of Silistra was one of the defining engagements of the Spring Campaigns on the Danube in 1854, and served as a major break after the winter lull of 1853-1854. The entire operation was marked by the decisiveness of the Russians who were almost desperate to gain a foothold within the Balkan regions of the Ottoman Empire. Towards the east, a Russian army numbering some 50,000 men – commanded by general Alexander Liders – crossed over from the Russian territories of Bessarabia and into the Ottoman-held Dobruja, occupying several strong points in the process. The combined Russian forces reached the famed "Trajan's Wall" by the beginning of April. This "wall" was a series of linear earthworks dating to Roman times, used at the time as a landmark and a territorial designation. But more importantly, it was situated just 30 miles (~49 kilometers) from the fortress of Silistra. As the forces of Liders were on the move, the other part of the Russian army, the central force commanded by Prince Gorchakov, crossed the Danube River and proceeded to lay siege to the fortress of Silistra.

This was an imposing strong point, and one "tough nut to crack". Between 12,000 and 18,000 Ottoman troops were heavily entrenched and ready to defend the fort, commanded by the seasoned Omar Pasha. And thanks to the works of the Prussian colonel Grach, the fortress was even more guarded than before, boasting a heavily protected inner Citadel with an outer ring of ten forts. The troops stationed there were perhaps not as formidable, being composed of Albanian and Egyptian troops, but they still boasted a favorable position. These soldiers were under the command of Ferik Musa Hulusi Pasha (who will be killed during the siege), and assisted by several (around six) British officers, including Captain James Butler and Lieutenant Charles Nasmyth. Both were seasoned veterans of the Ceylon Rifles company, serving in the East India Company Army and its actions.

Around April 5th, the Russian vanguard officially began the siege, creating entrenchments before Silistra. The vanguard was commanded by General Karl Schilder and Lieutenant-Colonel Eduard Totleben. The former already conquered Silistra once before, in 1829, relying at the time on extensive mining operations. However, this time it was his aide, Eduard Totleben, who was in charge of the entrenchments and the sapper works. But even so, the Russians were not able to fully encircle the town and fortress of Silistra, meaning that the Ottoman troops had a steady supply route to keep their garrison stocked. To that end, the Russian Field Marshal, Ivan Paskevich, personally arrived from Warsaw to Bucharest, taking direct control of the campaign and the siege of Silistra. Soon after, the first clashes began. On May 28th, following a sally, the Russians assaulted Fort Arab Tabia, a key outwork part of Silistra. The fort did fall – albeit briefly. After suffering heavy casualties and getting no relief, the Russians withdrew. General Dmitry Selvan was also one of these casualties, receiving a mortal wound during the assault. The Ottomans suffered as well: their commander, Musa Pasha, was killed by a shrapnel on June 2nd, and was hastily replaced by British officers, Nasmyth and Butler. Due to this, Ivan Paskevich claimed that foreign assistance (i.e. the two British officers) was an instrumental aid to the Ottomans, giving them superior strategic knowledge in their defense of Silistra. Another misfortune struck soon after: Ivan Paskevich claimed to have been hit with shrapnel on June 10th, when a shell burst close to him. It was likely that he wasn't seriously wounded, but he nevertheless chose to retire: at the time, Paskevich was 72 years old, and secretly doubted the whole campaign. He returned to Warsaw and his place was then taken by Prince Gorchakov. Further casualties just kept mounting. On June 13th, the leader of the vanguard, Karl Andreevich Schilder was also wounded, and died shortly afterwards in a field hospital. This left the Russians with one capable commander less. Even so, the outlying fort of Arab Tabia was finally captured on June 20th. On the very next morning, at 4am on June 21st, the Russian forces were preparing for the assault on the main fort at Silistra. However, a note was sent from Russia, directly from the Emperor Nicholas I, addressed to Ivan Paskevich. It said: *"The Siege of Silistra must be raised (stopped) if the fortress is not yet taken at the receipt of this letter. On June 13th 1854"*

The letter finally arrived to Paskevich just hours before the assault was to begin. Around 2am, as the troops were busily preparing for the assault, Prince Gorchakov received direct orders from Paskevich to raise the siege at once and to return to his position on the north side of the Danube River.

The reason for Nicholas I's order was a renewed threat from the western allies. He ordered a strategic retreat from Silistra because some 50,000 French and 20,000 British soldiers were concentrated close to the city of Varna. For these reasons, the siege of Silistra was abandoned. The Russian army withdrew across the Danube, destroying their bridge as they did so. The Ottoman army did not follow them. Here it is important to note that the Russian siege was not stopped because of Ottoman resistance. What is more, we cannot know what the outcome would have been if the Russians went through with their assault. The siege was actually stopped due to diplomatic pressures and a clear threat of military action and encirclement . Frightened by the Russian actions, the Austrians amassed troops on the borders with Wallachia and Moldavia, while the French and British amassed troops close to Varna. On June 27th , well over 20,000 British troops arrived at Varna, followed by 30,000 French soldiers under the command of Vice-Admiral Bruat, arriving on June 30th . This was now a very real threat for the Russians, and prompted their abandonment of the siege.

And now the situation on the Danubian frontline was rapidly changing. Even before these events, on February 27th, 1854, the British and the French demanded that the Russians were to withdraw from the occupied principalities of Wallachia and Moldavia. This was supported by the Austrians, who were now well aware that an intact Ottoman Empire served as a buffer zone between them and the slumbering giant that was the Russian Empire. However, Austria aimed to "stay out of it", but still refused to declare its neutrality, without declaring war on Russia. When the Russians rejected the ultimatum to withdraw, the British and the French entered the fray on the Ottoman side, and were now a present threat at Varna, causing Nicholas I to rethink his decision. And thus, after the retreat from Silistra and across the Danube, Nicholas I, Emperor of the Russians, acceded to the Austrian-Ottoman occupation of the Danubian Principalities of Wallachia and Moldavia, abandoning the occupation and signaling a quick end to the Danubian campaigns.

After the Russians withdrew their troops from the region, they were occupied by Austria for protection, and remained so during the war. Here it is important to note that once the Russians withdrew from the principalities, the original grounds for war were effectively removed. Yet even so, the hostilities continued, and the British and the French did not stop with the warfare. They were determined to once and for all solve the famed "Eastern Question", pertaining to the "sick man of Europe", and to eliminate the threat that the Russians posed to the Ottoman Empire. To that end, the western allies proposed, in August of 1854, the so-called "Four Points", that would build upon the Russian withdrawal from the Danube region and help end the Crimean War. These four points were:

- The Russian Empire had to abandon its protectorate of the Danubian principalities

- The Danube River had to be opened up for foreign commerce

- There had to be a revision of the "Straits Convention of 1841" (which only allowed the Ottoman and Russian warships within the Black Sea)

- Russia had to abandon all claims that allowed it to interfere in Ottoman affairs on behalf of Orthodox Christians

Of course, these four claims, largely one-sided in favor of the allies, required extensive negotiations – And Russia at once refused to negotiate on these matters. This was a cause for the British, Austrians, and French to continue their military actions against the Russian Empire, all in protection of the Ottoman Empire. To that end, they agreed that the invasion of the Crimean Peninsula, Russia's main access to the Black Sea, as a logical next step. And the war continued.

Yet even before the Russians managed to withdraw fully from the region, the Ottoman armies went on the pursuit. They entered the principalities and what ensued was a series of engagements between the two powers. One of the major such engagements was the battle of the Giurgiu fortress, known to the Ottomans as Yergëgu. The battle occurred on July 7th 1854 and was crucial in this part of the war. The Ottomans, led by Omar Pasha, descended upon the fort town of Giurgiu and conquered it with devastating effects. The battle had an infamous character – sadly – as the Ottoman troops proceeded to brutally massacre around 1,400 Russian wounded soldiers they captured here. Moreover, the fall of Giurgiu threatened Bucharest directly, the town where the Russian headquarters were. But by then, the Russian withdrawal was in full swing.

The Russian troops that were marching away from Wallachia and Moldavia were not alone in this. They were joined by thousands of Bulgarian peasants, who were eager to flee from the certain reprisals from the brutal Ottoman *bashi-bazouks*. Both before the Crimean War and after it, the world watched with shock as these irregular Turkish troops committed unspeakable atrocities against the Bulgarian villagers, and other Slavic peoples of the region. And now, the retreat of the Russians came as a big shock for all the oppressed Slavic peoples of the Balkans, who hoped for the victory of their Slavic Russian brethren. What is more, the retreat came as a shock for the Russian "slavophiles" at home, who envisioned the Russian war in the Danubian principalities as a war for the liberation of Slavs. To that end, the leading Russian pan-Slavic leader, Mikhail Petrovich Pogodin, continued to pressure the Russian Emperor Nicholas I to abandon the retreat and fight alone against the Western allies – an idea that was far from the realm of possible. By 7th September 1854, the Russian withdrawal was completed fully. The Austrians entered the principalities, acting as a "neutral peacekeeping force", and there were no further considerable conflicts in Wallachia and Moldavia from that point on.

The Unfolding Events in the Caucasus Region

Many historians agree that the Caucasus front of the Crimean War was in many ways a secondary front, largely overshadowed with the major events that transpired in the west. Yet even so, the things that transpired in the Caucasus were quite instrumental for the final outcome of the war, and worked to address some territorial and political questions between the Russian and Ottoman Empires that have not been answered in their previous wars.

The Caucasus of the period of the Crimean War could have been considered as one step behind the European theaters. This mountainous region, inhabited by diverse ethnicities adhering to either Islam or Christianity, was remote, hardly accessible, and often impassable. This affected communications (which were already limited in 1854), and it was often the case that events on the Western "fronts" influenced the actions in the Caucasus. Furthermore, there was a lot of military incompetence on both sides, and plenty of irregular formations that were noted for their aggressiveness.

In 1853, actions at Caucasus were characterized by four crucial events.

In the opening stages of the Crimean War, between 27th and 28th October 1853, the Ottomans acted by capturing the border fortress of Saint Nicholas close to Batumi (modern-day Georgia). Following this, they moved roughly 20,000 troops across the Cholok River, which served as a boundary between the two nations. In all regards, the

Russians were at a loss: they were outnumbered, threatened from land and sea, and distracted by the fighting with the Islamic insurgents of Imam Shamil. To that end, when the Ottomans moved beyond Batum, the Russians abandoned their coastal forts of Poti and Redut Kale, withdrawing back to Marani. Over the course of the next seven months, both sides in this part of the Caucasus were largely immobile. However, in the central part of the front, more crucial events transpired. The Ottomans moved northwards, from Ardahan towards Akhaltsike, awaiting reinforcements. In November, just a month after the official outbreak of the Crimean War, the Ottoman commander Ali Pasha at once launched an offensive, with the aim of capturing the strategically important Akhaltsike fortress. However, when the Ottoman army, numbering some 18,000 soldiers and 24 guns, neared the fortress, they were suddenly met with a Russian detachment commanded by Prince Ivan Andronnikov. The Russians numbered just 7,000 men. Yet even so, Andronnikov adopted an efficient strategy: he split his cavalry units into two columns. The first attacked the Ottomans head on, while the second swung to the side and flanked successfully. The ensuing battle was fierce and decisive, earning the Russians an important early victory. The Ottomans, thoroughly beaten, were forced to retreat back to their fortress city of Kars. In the end, the battlefield was strewn with roughly 4,000 dead Turks, and just 300 dead Russians. For the Ottomans, the defeat was a big wake up call, after which they stopped their offensive actions in the Trans-Caucasus region.

The next significant clash occurred near the town of Gyumri (historic Alexandropol), situated in modern Armenia. In November of 1853, the Ottomans moved around 30,000 troops eastwards towards this city, which was known as a major center of Russian troop movements. Crossing the state borders, the Ottomans established their artillery positions to the south of the city.

The Russian garrison at Gyumri was commanded by General-Lieutenant Prince Vasiliy Osipovich Bebutov, who had dispatched a sizeable force under the command of Prince Illiko (Ilya) Orbeliani to reconnoiter the area and protect the vulnerable Armenian villages from Ottoman irregulars. However, on November 14th, 1853, Prince Orbeliani soon met the Ottoman positions, facing heavy fire from their guns that were positioned on the strategic heights above the Village of Bayandur. The Prince was in a tough position, being unable to press an attack or to retreat without getting decimated. Around 1000 Russian soldiers fell victim to this encounter, with just 23 dead

Ottoman soldiers in comparison. However, the Ottomans did not press an attack on Orbeliani. And as the Ottomans failed to press their advantage, Prince Ilya Orbeliani was successfully rescued by the remaining Russian garrison, leaving the Ottomans to retire west. The historian W. E. D. Allen commented on this indecisive actions as follows:

"Bebutov had been lucky in extricating the ineffectual Orbeliani from a very dangerous situation, and Abdi Pasha had missed the opportunity of destroying the principal Russian field force in Transcaucasia at one blow in the first week of the campaign. Never was the inadequacy of the Turkish high command at this period more dramatically demonstrated."

It was now the Russian turn to take up the offensive. They chose to exploit the lack of Ottoman initiative, and went on a pursuit under the command of Vasili Bebutov. The reason why the Ottomans chose to abandon their positions at Bayandur heights was due to the approaching winter. The Ottoman commander Abdi Pasha feared that he lacked enough provisions to maintain defensive positions, so he chose to retreat back to the fortress of Kars. Bebutov at once went after him. What ensued was the decisive Battle of Başgedikler, fought on December 1st 1853. The Russian forces decisively beat the Ottomans in a hard battle, inflicting many casualties and seizing their provisions, supplies, and cannons. This defeat was a major setback for the Ottoman Empire, eliminating any chance of them seizing Caucasus at the start of the war. It also allowed the Russians to strengthen their positions in the area and to solidify their presence in the Caucasus.

Following the all-important Battle of Sinop, where Pavel Nakhimov obliterated the Ottoman fleet, and the other events of which we already wrote, the British and the French jointly declared war on Russia on January 3rd 1854. In the early stages of the Crimean War, the Anglo-French naval fleet first appeared in the waters of the Black Sea, forcing the Russians to abandon their "Black Sea Defensive Line" that stretched from Anapa to the south. At the same time, the famed and venerable Russian commander, Prince Mikhail Semyonovich Vorontsov, well in his late 70's, was replaced at his position by Nikolai Read. The new commander feared a combined Anglo-French landing, perhaps together with the insurgent armies of Imam Shamil of Dagestan. To that end, Nikolai Read suggested a complete withdrawal of the Russian armies north of the Caucasus mountains, a proposition for which he was promptly relieved of duties. He was replaced by the much more energetic and seasoned commander Aleksandr Baryatinsky.

In 1854, some of the notable events in the Caucasus theater included the forcing of the Ottoman troops back towards the city of Batum by Duke Georgiy Eristov, after his victories in two minor battles. Following this, Eristov stopped behind the boundary Cholok River, where he recuperated and rested his forces from June to the end of the year. There were successes in the far south of the theater as well. Commander Baron Karl Wrangel decisively pushed westwards, occupying Bayazit after a single battle.

Towards the center of the front, however, a much more important event occurred in August 1854. It was the Battle of Kurekdere, fought on August 6th, a clash that ended in a major Russian victory. Following the major defeat at Başgedikler, the bruised and demoralized Ottomans were holed up in their fortress at Kars. Abdi Pasha, the commander who was blamed for the defeat and poor conduct, left his armies in a very poor state. During the winter of 1853-1854, around

20,000 soldiers perished through disease and malnutrition. And when the spring came, he was replaced by the inexperienced Zarif Mustafa Pasha, the new field marshal. Sadly, the new commander had almost zero experience in this role, and was under constant pressure by the high command to finally confront the Russian armies in the Caucasus and beat them. However, Zarif Mustafa Pasha was very indecisive and passive: he failed to use his chances and strike against the Russians when opportunities arose – even when he was urged to do so by his aides. Because of this, the Russian army had all the confidence they needed – they moved freely across the landscape and in the vicinity of Kars, waiting for the right opportunity to strike against the enemy. What ensued was a series of maneuvers and incredible incompetence displayed by the Ottoman commander Zarif Pasha. He repeatedly staved off his attack, missing many chances and neglecting the advice of his officers. When he did dare to attack the encamped Russian armies, he made numerous errors. By poorly coordinating his divisions, he completely lost the element of surprise on which he counted. To that end, his armies arrived into position to face an already alarmed and ready Russian army in full battle formations. The Ottomans numbered some 40,000 men compared to just 28,000 soldiers on the Russian side. Yet even so, the battle was a total Ottoman blunder. Panic and confusion marked their movements, and the Russian command had an easy job of utterly defeating them. In the end, the entire Ottoman army broke and fled in panic to the fortress of Kars. It was a major Russian victory, and proof that the Ottoman Empire was thoroughly unable to defeat the Russians in the Caucasus all on their own. Zarif Pasha was at once summoned to Istanbul, where he was put on trial for his atrocious military conduct. To that end, the Battle of Kurekdere was one of the foremost events in the Caucasus of the year 1854, and was one of the first battles of the war to receive substantial news coverage abroad. One of the leading correspondents for "The Times" newspapers, Humphry Sandwith, was actually present at the battle and was able to leave a detailed and lasting impression of the affair for the readers in Europe and in Britain. He wrote:

"With a vivid impression of the whole engagement, from the first cannon shot to the last straggling discharges of musketry, I can use no language too strong to express my reprobation of the conduct of nearly four-fifths of the Turkish officers present. In accounting for the defeat of an army numbering nearly 40,000 men of all arms by a hostile force of less than one-half that number, it is not sufficient to say that the management of the whole battle on the side of the Turks was a series of blunders from first to last; strategical errors might have protracted the engagement, and have added to the cost of a victory, but downright cowardice alone – which no generalship could have redeemed – gave the day to the Russians. One arm, and one arm only behaved well – the artillery – which, with its commander, Tahir Pasha, acted worthily of any army in Europe. Of the whole 40 battalions of infantry two regiments – the 5th Anatolian and 4th Desartet – alone stood their ground and resisted cavalry. Three successive times did three squadrons of Russian dragoons bear down upon these exceptionally brave regiments with a force before which many better disciplined troops would have yielded, without effecting an opening in their ranks; and it was only after a fourth charge, supported by the fire of a field-piece, that they gave way, when only 250 of the first and 400 of the second escaped death from the Russian sabres. Than the conduct of the rest of the infantry, nothing could well be worse, except that of the entire cavalry, which would have disgraced the rawest Bashi-Bazouks. If such, however, was the conduct of the men, that, as I have said, of the great majority of the superior officers was still more infamous. An hour after the action began, there was hardly a Bunbashi (major) or Murallai (colonel) to be seen; almost to a man they had deserted their regiments, and fled back to the camp to secure their baggage and send it off to Kars. Battalion upon battalion, and squadron upon squadron, were thus left without leaders – a status quo, among others, which mainly contributed to the general confusion and ultimate defeat."

From all this, we understand that the Battle of Kurekdere was one of the major Ottoman defeats in the Crimean War, and an incredible blunder from start to finish. It might have changed fully the chain of events in the Caucasus, and still we are left imagining what possible outcome of the war would have been if the Ottoman army was commanded by someone more competent than the inexperienced Zarif Pasha.

Elsewhere on the Caucasian Front, the Russians had to face the Islamic rebels, irregulars under the command of Imam Shamil. These warriors – the hardy tribesmen of the Caucasian mountains – connected with the Turkish troops with the aim of attacking the Russian army stationed in Georgia and Circassia. Throughout July 1854, Imam Shamil launched a great attack on the Russians in Georgia, advancing all the way towards the capital of Tbilisi, defended only by a Russian garrison that numbered some 2,000 men. However, the Ottomans – largely affected by their defeats at Bayandur and Başgedikler, and the indecisiveness of the Zarif Pasha – failed to provide any assistance to their allies under Shamil. To that end, without support, the latter failed to seize his chance and had to withdraw his troops back into the mountainous region of Dagestan.

Meanwhile, the British and the French were not willing to abandon the war cause, even after the Russians withdrew from the occupied Danubian principalities, and even after they were plagued by a string of hardships. Throughout the summer of 1854, due to atrocious sanitary conditions, an epidemic of cholera broke out amongst the allied troops, claiming many lives. An added blow for the allies' morale occurred on August 10th, when a huge fire erupted within Varna (where the troops were stationed), heavily damaging the allied supply base. These sanitary and logistical issues continued all the way until the end of the Crimean War. Due to these factors, especially the cholera and the dwindling supplies, the allied command understood that the troops had to move from Varna. However, the British government refused to retreat, considering that the Russian withdrawal from the Danube "was no justification for all the victims up to that point", and how they were "not ready to negotiate about a peace until the Russian forces remain untouched". Sir James Graham, Britain's First Lord of the Admiralty, had his initial military strategy – pertaining to the destruction of the Russian naval bases – flared up by the British press, and was even supported by Napoleon III. To that end, the destruction of the Russian Black Sea fleet that was stationed in Sevastopol became the symbolic goal of the final victory of the allies in the Crimean War.

The War Proper: Crimean Campaigns of 1854

As the winter of 1854 was approaching, the allied sights remained firmly fixed on the Russian naval stronghold of Sevastopol. Knocking it out of the game would severely shake the Russian Empire and its power, and potentially force it out of the war and end the pretensions on the Ottoman Empire territories. However, the allies had to act fast. Due to the nearing winter and the inadequate strategic preparations, their high command decided on a sudden attack on the port of Sevastopol, which was situated on the southwestern point of the Crimean Peninsula. Landing from the sea, the allied forces had to be swift and decisive, since they would be then facing the entire inland of the Crimean peninsula – and all the Russian armies within it. To that end, they had to be sure that they had a strong foothold and to secure their flanks. Because of this, it was decided to first conquer the city of Eupatoria, the only safe harbor in this southern region of the peninsula. On July 20th 1854, British and French officers and engineers sailed as close as possible to Sevastopol on the ship HMS Fury. Their goal: survey the harbor and the Russian positions in order to get an idea what awaited the invading party. The ship succeeded in nearing the harbor, whereupon they observed heavy coastal batteries and formations. In their reports, it was suggested that some 15,000 to 20,000 Russian troops were encamped there. And as the high command now had some knowledge of the enemy strengths, the plans could continue. A great allied fleet was assembled, carrying horses, supplies, ammo, and siege equipment. In September of 1854, the grand Crimean campaign finally began – and in style. A massive fleet of 360 ships in seven columns sailed towards Crimea, commanded by Lord Ragland and General St. Arnaud. They headed from Varna across to the Calamita Bay, anchoring at Eupatoria on 14th September, some 50 kilometers north of Sevastopol. And when such a massive force landed at this town, its surrender was quick to follow. The muslim Crimean Tatar populace, making up at that time some 80% of the entire population of Crimea, at once rebelled against the Russians and organized armed gangs that would aid the invading Allies.

The Russian population on the other hand, began fleeing northwards in panic, instilling fear in the Russian troops that came from the direction of Perekop – the only land connection to the continent.

Before the landing even occurred, the Russians were not prepared. Both Ivan Paskevich and Menshikov – at the time the commander of the Russian troops in Crimea – warned the Emperor Nicholas I about the probable allied expedition to Crimea, but they later dismissed the possibility due to the arriving winter. And with having no leads about the possible landing site, Menshikov took no precautions to prevent an allied disembarking. Due to this, the British and the French had no contest when arriving at Crimea: their force of some 63,000 men and 128 cannons calmly marched towards Sevastopol in a line that was 6 kilometers long. On September 19th, as the allies reached the River Bulganak, the first minor skirmish with the Russian occurred, between the light English cavalry and the Russian Cossak troops.

Initially, Menshikov's plan of defense was based on the concentration of his troops in defense of Alma, the last strategically important natural barrier that prevented the allied approach to Sevastopol. However, with the new events unfolding, Menshikov feared a second allied landing on Kerch or Feodosia, and thus he kept most of his troops in reserve. The clash at Alma was expected, yet the allies had more than a half of troops that Menshikov had. Still, the latter thought that due to his defensive positions on the Alma Heights, and the support of 116 guns, the Russians were to gain victory and slow the allied advance for at least three weeks until their reinforcements would arrive.

On September 20th, the Battle of Alma ensued, and was quick to crush Menshikov's dreams of victory. In this decisive clash, the Russians under Alexander Menshikov had some 37,500 troops, while the combined allied forces of the British, French, and the Ottomans had some 56,500 troops. And the allies didn't just have the advantage of numbers, they also had support from the war ships and a new and deadly weapon: the Minié rifle. Minié rifles fired the eponymous Minié ball, a new type of bullet adopted around 1847. The Minié cylindrical pointed bullet had a range of 1,600 meter and much higher firepower than usual, which gave the allies an important upper hand in the conflict. Also adopted was a new battle line: the so-called *Thin Red Line* which relied on just two parallel lines of soldiers. This gave the Minié rifles an advantage and better efficiency. In comparison, the Russians still relied on their thick line movements, which was both a tactical and operative disadvantage at the time. The Battle of Alma lasted for five hours. Throughout the clash, the allies made a series of disjointed attacks, and several feats that came totally unexpected for the Russians. Notably, the French attacked and "turned" (collapsed) the Russian left flank with an attack up and along steep cliffs that the Russians considered unscalable. In the meanwhile, the British waited to see the outcome of the French daring attack, and as support attempted to assault the Russian main positions. Twice they were unsuccessful, but they eventually gained the upper hand thanks to the precise and devastating rifle fire with the Minié balls. Eventually, both Russian flanks collapsed, and the center followed: the Russian troops broke and fled in panic, leaving the allies victorious. And just two hours later, after some reorganizing, the allied troops continued their march towards Sevastopol. A surviving letter from the time records the decisiveness of the Allied advance:

"Five days later the three armies marched south to meet the Russian force that waited on the newly fortified heights above the river Alma, blocking their way to Sevastopol. That evening the cavalry engaged in a brief and indecisive skirmish at the Bulganek River. The next day, 20th September, with great courage and much loss of life, the Allied armies stormed the heights of Alma, driving the Russians from a position that their commander Menshikov had boasted he could hold for three weeks. So confident was he that he had invited several aristocratic ladies to picnic with him and watch the battle below. In the event, they joined the Russian army in their ignominious flight back to Sevastopol, one leaving her petticoat behind in her panic."

The Russians retreated into the city of Sevastopol, awaiting the inevitable. Even though the initial allied plan was meant to attack the city from the northern side, some last minute changes had to be made. This was due to the false information received from Crimean Tatar sources which said that the southern side of the city is almost undefended, and also due to the fact that Alexander Menshikov decided to block the approach to Sevastopol harbor by sinking five ships and two frigates. To that end, the allied high command decided to attack from the south, where their ships could land at ports of Balaclava (for the British) and the Kamiesch (for the French), each one supporting their troops respectively. However, it would later appear that this decision to change the attack plan was a serious blunder. The southern attack meant that the allies couldn't effectively disrupt and block the Russian supply routes into the city, which was a crucial element of the initial plan. Furthermore, the allies overlooked the fact that the southern defensive fortifications of Sevastopol were much better and stronger than the others. Yet even so, the Siege of Sevastopol, one of the foremost events of the entire Crimean War, began. The allies made camp and awaited further supplies and reinforcements from Varna, all the while preparing to bombard the city. The Russians on the other hand, frantically worked to fortify their defensive positions on the south side. The foremost commanders that were in command of the defense of Sevastopol were Vice Admiral Vladimir Kornilov, commander of the harbor Vice Admiral Pavel Nakhimov, and the noted engineer, General Graf Eduard von Totleben. The latter famously put into action the entire populace of Sevastopol, from sailors, commoners, women (including prostitutes), and even war prisoners, directing them all in the building of defenses, barricades, and digging of trenches.

In the meantime, according to the Allied strategic plan and the preparations of the siege, the allied combined army was split into two corps – the siege corps with the task of attacking Russian forts; and the scout corps with the task of guarding the allied right flank from the possible attack by the Russians.

By mid-October, the allies had some 120 guns prepared to bombard the city, while the defending Russians had about *three times as many*. Nevertheless, the allies began their first bombing of the city, both from land and sea, on October 16th. The attackers were optimistic, thinking that Sevastopol was to fall after just a few hours. However, the bombing would last until October 25th. In the exchange of cannon shots from both sides, several critical hits were scored. The first of these hits was made by the Russians: they bombarded a French ammo magazine, completely silencing their guns. But soon after, on the first day of the bombing, the British fire scored a direct hit on the Russian magazines stored in the Malakoff redoubt. A devastating explosion was created, which created a major gap in the city's defenses and also killed the commander, Admiral Kornilov. Even with this hit, the British and the French did not press the initiative, thus missing the chance to end the siege early on. This led to a prolonged siege. All in all, the Siege of Sevastopol lasted 349 days in total, from 17th October 1854, until 11th September 1855.

A Clash Etched in History: The Battle of Balaclava

After the end of the very first day of the bombardment, the Russian commander Menshikov decided to crush the allied siege by conducting a direct attack on Balaclava. The latter was the British main command and supply base. However, it had a flaw, one which Menshikov recognized. The flaw was this: by disembarking at Balaclava, the port that lay to the west of Kamiesch – where the French were based – the British forces under Lord Raglan *had* to commit a part of their forces in protecting the French right flank. This was a major thinning of their lines, as Ragland simply had insufficient troops for the task. Menshikov sought to use this exposure: he gave command of some 25,000 men to General Pavel Liprandi, hoping to strike the British at Balaclava and completely disrupt their supply lines towards Sevastopol.

The British had sporadic intelligence indications that the Russian attack at Balaclava was inevitable. After each and every report and suspicion the British received – which turned out to be false alarms – Lord Raglan had to react. However, after a few of these false alarms, he failed to act, believing that he was needlessly exhausting the men. But the report on October 25th was no false alarm, as the British would later realize. Because at early dawn, around 05 am, the Russian forces under General Liprandi assembled and marched out in the murky pre-dawn light towards the valley at Balaclava. And in the small village of Kamara, just outside of Balaclava, was the most forward of the British sentry outposts, the so-called "vedettes". These were under the command of Lord George Bingham, the 3rd Earl of Lucan, the British Commander of the Cavalry Division. And were they in for a surprise! For the soldiers that stood on sentry watch in that murky dawn, the appearance of slowly approaching Russian Cossacks and mounted *uhlans* was certainly a shock. These were the leading elements of the Russian army, moving up steadily under the cover of darkness. However, some reports state that the sentries didn't even see the Cossacks. It was the duty field officer for that day, Captain Alexander Low of the 4th Light Dragoons, that spotted the approaching columns, raising the alarm, giving the sentry troops at Kamara a chance to retreat and regroup. In the meantime, Lord Lucan, the commander of the British, went on his daily inspection of the troops, redoubts, and outposts, with his staff in tow: Major Thomas McMahon, Lord George Paget, and Lord William Paulet. While inspecting, they approached the positions at the site called "Canrobert's Hill", not knowing that the Russian vanguard was already assembled there, with cannons pointing directly to these positions.

So it was that when Lucan and his staff approached the positions, they could faintly observe two fluttering signal flags belonging to the Russians. The realization of what was happening came abruptly and with a great surprise. Lord Paged, who was the commanding officer of the 4th Light Dragoons, left a curious memory of that moment:

> *"Hello," said Lord William, "there are two flags flying; what does it mean?" "Why, that surely is the signal that the enemy is approaching," said Major McMahon. "Are you quite sure?" we replied. Hardly were the words out of McMahon's mouth, when bang went a cannon from the redoubt in question, fired on the advancing masses of the enemy.*

For the British forces, one of the vital lifelines around Balaclava was the so-called "Woronzoff Road", which ran along the ridge of the Causeway Heights. This provided a crucial communication line for the British, as it was the only firm road that connected the siege works around Sevastopol with the command at Balaclava. All around the aforementioned Causeway Heights that lay in front of Balaclava, Ottoman troops were engaged in the frantic building of six defensive redoubts, which were meant to defend the port and the Woronzoff road. However, the work on the redoubts was far from done, and only nine twelve pounder naval guns were used to protect the positions. This left the ill-equipped Ottoman troops to face the Russians at these positions, giving them little chance of staving off the assault. The Ottomans stationed at Redoubt Number One at Canrobert's Hill numbered 500, and bore the brunt of the Russian might. One report states:

> *"The Turks, although greatly outnumbered, made a gallant stand, and both Lord Lucan and Sir Colin Campbell manifested their approval!*

The former called out to me 'Blunt, those Turks are doing well!' but, having lost fully one-third of their number, and, expecting no support, they retired leaving their three guns, their killed and a few prisoners, most of them wounded, in the enemy's hands."

Out of 500 men at the first redoubt, 400 were casualties. Heavy bombardment obliterated the garrison. All the while, the British commander Lord Raglan could observe the obvious threat to Balaclava and his vital communications from his field headquarters located on Sapouné Heights. He also knew that the only British troops that stood between Balaclava and the oncoming Russian storm were just two British Cavalry brigade: the Light Brigade and the Heavy Brigade, both encamped in the Balaclava Valley. Also available was a small infantry force of the 93rd Highlanders. These formations were become immortalized for their activities at the Battle of Balaclava, notably the episodes known as *"The Charge of the Light Brigade"*, and the *"Thin Red Line"*.

Lord Raglan issued orders for additional troops to rush down to the valley in support of the cavalry brigades. He ordered the Second and Fourth British Divisions to break camp around the Sevastopol Siege lines and to reinforce the Balaclava positions. Alas, there was significant delay: the divisional commanders didn't want to make the trip to the valley, especially since their troops were terribly exhausted after spending the night in the trenches and marching the previous day. However, they were soon on the march, realizing of the Russian threat and the Ottoman defeat at the Number One Redoubt. In the meantime, as the Russian infantry swarmed over the Ottoman-built redoubts, some 3,000 Russian cavalrymen made a daring move, shifting from the North part of the valley onto the Causeway heights, attempting to advance southwards and occupy Balaclava. At the very same time, the British Heavy Cavalry Brigade, of some 900 mounted men commanded by Major General James Scarlett, moved eastwards, also towards the south part of the valley. And now, Lord Raglan could see with his staff, looking from high ground, that the Russian cavalry and the British Heavy Cavalry Brigade were inevitably converging. However, they could not see each other initially, until the Russians came over the Causeway heights, beginning their move into the southern valley where the British heavy cavalry awaited. The two forces clash in an episode that became known as the "Charge of the Heavy Brigade". It was a decisive success for the British who managed to inflict heavy losses on the Russian cavalry in just 10 minutes of fighting.

At the same time, while the Russian cavalry moved across the Causeway Heights, some four squadrons of its main force detached and headed directly towards Balaclava. However, they soon found an obstacle in their path: the famed 93rd Highlanders commanded by Sir Colin Campbell. These soldiers were supported by two Turkish battalions, but these promptly fled once they saw the Russians coming onwards. But the Highlanders stood their ground. Their commander, Campbell, formed them up into a line that was just two man deep – a tactic that was not common at the time. Those observing from the high grounds could only see a "thin red line tipped with steel", the expression used by the *Times* correspondent William Russel, and one that would catch on for good. This brave line of highlanders stood in the face of the approaching Russian cavalry. It took great courage to stand your ground while war horses rushed towards you. But the highlanders stood. It is stated that their commander addressed them with these words: *"There is no retreat from here, men. You must die where you stand."* His aide, John Scott, is said to have replied, *"Aye, Sir Colin. If needs be, we'll do that."* The regiment then fired one volley from some 900 yards, at once sending the Russians fleeing. Some sources state that they fired two volleys, before the Russians broke and fled, abandoning their intent to take Balaclava. The event became a sensation back home in England, and was promptly "lionized" in order to boost morale and to fix the already negative image of the war with the citizens. It was subsequently called the "Thin Red Line", and is now used as a symbol for the unwavering British composure in battle, even under great pressure.

But the far more popular event of the Battle of Balaclava is of course the immortalized "Charge of the Light Brigade". Considered by many historians as the single, most unfortunate event in the history of the British military, the charge of the Light Cavalry Brigade was the result of discontent amongst officers, and the misinterpretation of direct orders. While the Heavy Brigade was engaging the Russian cavalry in their own charge, the Light Brigade was positioned at the western end of the North valley. They stood in their positions when the decimated Russian cavalry that fled after their defeat in the skirmish with the Heavy Brigade rushed past. It was a clear opportunity for the Light Brigade to hunt them down and finish them off – but the chance was not used. Instead, the retreating Russian cavalry continued onwards to take up positions behind a battery of eight cannons at the far end of the North Valley. And that's where the great mistake occurred. Observing from the heights, Lord Raglan spotted Russian troops on the Causeway Heights – at the other end of the valley – trying to remove the captured Turkish naval guns. This was a major threat, and the only available squadron to deal with it was the Light Brigade. To that end, Lord Raglan issued an order, which General Airey wrote down for the commander of the Light Brigade, Lord Lucan. The order stated:

"Lord Raglan wishes the cavalry to advance rapidly to the front, and try to prevent the enemy carrying away the guns. Troop of horse artillery may accompany. French cavalry is on your left. Immediate."

This was an urgent order, and had to be delivered to the Light Brigade as soon as possible. To that end, it was entrusted to the young Captain Lewis Nolan. Many agreed that this was a very poor choice, since

Nolan would later be considered as the foremost accused for the fiasco of the Light Brigade. The young officer rode promptly to deliver the written order of Lord Raglan. He offered it to Lord Lucan, with whom he had strained relations at best, and the order made little sense to him. This was because the guns in question, situated on the Causeway Heights, could not be seen from the valley floor where Lucan and his brigade were positioned. Reportedly, Lucan needed clarification, asking Lewis Nolan which enemy and which guns was Raglan referring to. The story states that Nolan, energetic and insolent, flung his arm out in the direction of the retreating Russian cavalry and the guns they stood behind, saying "*There is your enemy. There are your guns, my lord.*" This was a clear result of the pre-existing antagonism between these two officers, and a major blunder. Raglan's original order was not understood, while Lucan was irked and did not want to discuss it further with the insolent young Nolan. To that end, Lord Lucan instructed the commanding officer, Cardigan, to assemble and charge directly into the Russian cavalry and the cannons at the end of the North valley. Disaster followed.

Roughly 666 cavalrymen rode off at full gallop into certain death. Lord Raglan and his staff, positioned on the heights of Sapouné Hill, could only watch in absolute horror, as the order was completely misunderstood. Facing direct fire from the Russian guns, the light brigade was decimated. Of the 666 men known to have rode, 271 became casualties. Of these 110 men were killed, 129 were wounded, and another 32 wounded were taken prisoner. On top of that, 375 horses were killed as well. It was a carnage in every sense of the word. Decimated and unable to capture the Russian guns, the brigade withdrew back to its positions. The whole affair was observed by the "*Times*" correspondent William Russell, who wrote the following excerpt, shocked by what he saw:

"At 11:00 our Light Cavalry Brigade rushed to the front... The Russians opened on them with guns from the redoubts on the right, with volleys of musketry and rifles. They swept proudly past, glittering in the morning sun in all the pride and splendor of war. We could hardly believe the evidence of our senses. Surely that handful of men were not going to charge an army in position? Alas! It was but too true—their desperate valor knew no bounds, and far indeed was it removed from its so-called better part—discretion. They advanced in two lines, quickening the pace as they closed towards the enemy. A more fearful spectacle was never witnessed than by those who, without the power to aid, beheld their heroic countrymen rushing to the arms of sudden death. At the distance of 1200 yards the whole line of the enemy belched forth, from thirty iron mouths, a flood of smoke and flame through which hissed the deadly balls. Their flight was marked by instant gaps in our ranks, the dead men and horses, by steeds flying wounded or riderless across the plain. The first line was broken—it was joined by the second, they never halted or checked their speed an instant. With diminished ranks, thinned by those thirty guns, which the Russians had laid with the most deadly accuracy, with a halo of flashing steel above their heads, and with a cheer which was many a noble fellow's death cry, they flew into the smoke of the batteries; but ere they were lost from view, the plain was strewed with their bodies and with the carcasses of horses. They were exposed to an oblique fire from the batteries on the hills on both sides, as well as to a direct fire of musketry. Through the clouds of smoke we could see their sabers flashing as they rode up to the guns and dashed between them, cutting down the gunners as they stood. The blaze of their steel, like an officer standing near me said, "was like the turn of a shoal of mackerel." We saw them riding through the guns, as I have said; to our delight, we saw them returning, after breaking through a column of Russian infantry and scattering them like chaff, when the flank fire of the battery on the hill swept them down, scattered and broken as they were. Wounded men and dismounted troopers flying towards us told the sad tale—demigods

could not have done what they had failed to do. At the very moment when they were about to retreat, a regiment of lancers was hurled upon their flank. Colonel Shewell, of the 8th Hussars, saw the danger and rode his men straight at them, cutting his way through with fearful loss. The other regiments turned and engaged in a desperate encounter. With courage too great almost for credence, they were breaking their way through the columns which enveloped them, where there took place an act of atrocity without parallel in modern warfare of civilized nations. The Russian gunners, when the storm of cavalry passed, returned to their guns. They saw their own cavalry mingled with the troopers who had just ridden over them, and to the eternal disgrace of the Russian name, the miscreants poured a murderous volley of grape and canister on the mass of struggling men and horses, mingling friend and foe in one common ruin. It was as much as our Heavy Cavalry Brigade could do to cover the retreat of the miserable remnants of that band of heroes as they returned to the place they had so lately quitted in all the pride of life. At 11:35 not a British soldier, except the dead and dying, was left in front of those bloody Muscovite guns ..."

In the end, the Battle of Balaclava was indecisive. Following the final "Charge of the Light Brigade", the Russian forces soon withdrew. The British and the French forces had no chance of pursuing and continuing the fight. The utter decimation of their light cavalry brigade was an extremely traumatic shock for all present, and the British remained inactive for the remainder of the day. Furthermore, if Lord Raglan did press on the pursuit, he would have exposed his vulnerable supply base at Balaclava to further Russian attacks.

For the Russians, however, the battle was considered a victory. The morale of the Russian troops was immensely boosted, since considerable gains were made from the effort. The Russians captured the redoubts and the guns on them, and also gained control of the Worontsoff Road, a fact that severely restricted allied movements.

Still, the Battle of Balaclava was instrumental in several regards. Chiefly, it allowed the Russian commander Menshikov to spot an obvious weakness of the allies. This was their lack of men: their siege lines around Sevastopol were stretched out so much that Lord Raglan hardly had enough men to man all the positions. And Menshikov was eager to exploit that fault. To that end, just a few days after the devastating battle at Balaclava, the Russians under Menshikov launched another attack, this time across the Tchernaya River. Fought on November 4th, 1854, it became known as the Battle of Inkerman, and was much bloodier and costly than the one that preceded it. At Inkerman, the Russians had a significant numerical advantage: around 40,500 of their troops squared off against just 15,700 allied soldiers. Yet even so, the allies held their ground. This battle was noted for the atrocious weather conditions: fog and rain reduced visibility, and thick mists cut off many of the squadrons and regiments. Due to this fact, Battle of Inkerman was known as the "Soldier's Battle", due to many *ad hoc* and haphazard formations and counter attacks that were done on the lowest unit level. This battle was bloody and devastating, putting to the test the skills and perseverance of all soldiers. And even though being outnumbered, the allies managed to gain an upper hand. In the end, the Russians withdrew from the battle, their attack ending in failure. The allies had some 5,000 killed and wounded, while the Russians had as much as 11,000 killed men. The defeat at Inkerman completely broke the will of the Russians and showed them that they will have no more chances to defeat the allies in the field, and that the next stop is the Siege of Sevastopol. Furthermore, the Battle of Inkerman remains a great legacy of the British army, and a testament to the tenacity of the British soldier in face of overwhelming odds.

However, just nine days after Inkerman, on November 14th, a new misfortune struck the allies: The Great Storm of 1854. On this day, Crimea was engulfed in a severe storm that caused great damage for the allied fleets. The storm swept in and around the Black Sea, greatly disrupting maritime routes. It was one of the fiercest storms in recent memory – a true wrath of nature. At the time, the allied – British and French – fleets were anchored outside their ports in Crimea. The reason they were anchored outside the ports was fear of a new Russian attack. Most of these were supply vessels, carrying all the necessary stocks for the winter campaigns. The storm came unexpectedly and with great ferocity. Trees were uprooted from the grounds, tents and shacks leveled. But the fleet was the most vulnerable, and suffered greatly. Some 37 ships of the allied fleet were either totally wrecked and sunk, or heavily damaged. As a result, a great deal of the winter supplies were lost. These included the much needed fuel and food, and the winter uniforms. And that was not a good thing. Even before the onset of winter, conditions amongst all the parties at war were dreadful. Disease and malnutrition were rampant, and supplies were crucial. As a result of the storm, many soldiers suffered greatly throughout the winter, with thousands of lives being lost to hypothermia, hunger, and disease. Another great loss for the allies was in ammunition. With the ships that were lost was also around 10 million rounds of the all-important Minie bullets. Furthermore, a series of scandals shook British society as a direct result of the storm. Many faults surfaced: the storm already thundered across Europe, but no warning was sent to the allied fleets even so. Also, a scandal involved the disappearance of a great sum of money, which was raised voluntarily as a help for the troops, but was stolen by the officers instead. Of course, as a result of the storm, much of the action was suspended throughout the winter months. The roads around Sevastopol were turned into impassable muddy rivers, and allied engineers had to work day and night to make them operational again. All in all, the Great Storm of 1854 was a major setback for everyone. No one ever got to measure the scale and strength of the storm, but modern research and estimates suggest that the speeds of the wind at the time were around force 11 on the Beaufort Scale.

And the following months brought the suffering of the soldiers in the Crimean War to the watchful eye of the public. Greater efforts were made to thoroughly change battlefield medicine and surgery, to fight for the rights of the common soldier, and to bring to the public attention the misery that reigned "on the ground". A great helper to this cause was, again, William Howard Russell, the "Times" correspondent who saw firsthand the horrors and the dreadful conditions during the winter of 1854-1855. He wrote:

"The wounded were carried to the ships and transported to the barracks at Scutari, where they now lie. This vast building is admirably adapted to the purpose, and, as the supply of surgeons is larger than has hitherto been though necessary in war, the sufferers may so far be considered well off. But their number, which, including the wounded, and the cholera and fever patients, cannot be less than 4,000, would be beyond the capacity of almost any medical staff. The proportion of surgeons falls still very far below the standard of any ordinary hospital. It is barely enough, if enough, for operations, and for the worst cases. It is not enough for that regular, close, and delicate attention which is absolutely necessary in many cases for the cure as well as for the comfort of the patient. Thus we are told of patients lying for hours, and even days, and making desperate attempts to catch the surgeon in his flying visits from ward to ward. This great deficiency, great as it is, can scarcely be called the greatest. There are no nurses at Scutari; at least, none for the English, though the French are attended by some Sisters of Mercy from a neighboring convent."

William Russell's war correspondency was revolutionary in many ways. His detailed reports of the disorganized and miserable state of the British army in Crimea had a profound impact on the British public opinion. The latter blamed Lord Raglan and the ministers of the British government for this condition. The public uproar had both direct and indirect influence in the matter. And thanks to that public cry for a much needed reform of the health aid, the British government approved the dispatch of nurses onto the battlefield and an organized dispatch of Florence Nightingale and some 30 additional nurses into the military British base at Scutari, close to Istanbul. Here, a hospital for the admission of the wounded and ill soldiers was created.

The Deciding Factor: The Siege of Sevastopol

The all-important question of supplies was also bothering the Russians too, especially now that the winter found them within the confines of Sevastopol – besieged. The lack of a railway system caused great problems for the Russians throughout the Crimean War. And due to the fact that the allies were overseeing the Black Sea, the Russians had to conduct their supply by horse cart – across the muddy trails of southern Russia. Because of this, malnutrition, disease, and lack of crucial winter equipment was also a huge problem for them – just as it was for the allies. Furthermore, the concentration of the Ottoman troops near the port of Eupatoria was a major threat to cut off Crimea from the Russian mainland, and it also threatened the Russian supply route through Perekop – the only land route in or out of Crimea. Eupatoria lay some 75 kilometers to the North of Sevastopol, and Emperor Nicholas I was quick to recognize the great threat that the loss of this port could bring. To that end, he wrote to Prince Menshikov in December 1854, demanding that the arriving reinforcements and supplies were to be put to good use, expressing his fears that Crimea could easily be cut off if the Ottoman troops at Eupatoria were left unchecked. Prince Menshikov understood the substantiated fears of Emperor Nicholas, and took the necessary preparations to assault Eupatoria, either to destroy it or hold it. He informed his officers in Crimea that the Emperor *insisted* on the capture of Eupatoria, and said that he had been authorized to use and rely on the reinforcements currently en route to Crimea from Russia. However, Menshikov himself was not to lead the attack on Eupatoria. He went on to select a commanding officer, but his first two choices were quick to decline the task, citing several excuses in order to avoid leading the attack in which they had doubt at the onset. In the end, Menshikov had to settle for an artillery staff officer, Lieutenant General Stepan Khrulev, whom he described as "willing to do exactly what you tell him". The man was to lead the attack on Eupatoria. Still, the task at hand was immense. Largely inexperienced in leading great battles, General Stepan Khrulev was facing off against the seasoned Omer Pasha Latas. Before proceeding with the attack, Khrulev relied on thorough reconnaissance. After several observations, it was understood that Eupatoria was almost completely surrounded by defensive fortifications, earthworks, and ditches. However, one section of the wall seemed unfinished, and Khrulev hoped that he could break through at that point – it was his only chance. Thus the battle of Eupatoria occurred, on February 17th 1855. Khrulev advanced in the dusk, his movements obscured by the half-light and the lay of the land. His troops – some 19,000 men and 108 cannons – were spread into three columns. Khrulev wanted the two side columns to flank left and right respectively, and thus lead away the Ottoman troops from the center, where the main column was supposed to break through. Furthermore, the general hoped for an element of surprise, but did not get one: the Ottomans expected an attack at Eupatoria, knowing all too well of the threat they made. To that end, when the Russians reached the town walls, the Ottomans were already fully alert. Yet even so, the attack proceeded. Heavy exchange of cannon fire on both sides ensued for about an hour, and Khrulev personally led the attack of the left flank. However, once the troops reached the ditches before Eupatoria, they realized that there was no way through: water filled the deep ditches and made for an impassable obstacle. The siege equipment could not be implemented - the Russians were at a dead end. Seeing his dire situation, Khrulev rationally decided on a full retreat. Eupatoria remained in Ottoman hands.

The defeat did not sit right back home in Russia. The Emperor Nicholas I was filled with despair, depression, and disappointment, with his spirits seemingly broken. Already frail of health at the time, he caught a chill and caught pneumonia. He refused all medical treatment, which some decirbed as passive suicide. Either way, the emperor died soon after, on March 2nd 1855. He was succeeded on the throne by his son, Emperor Alexander II, who was quick to dismiss both Menshikov and Khrulev, and to continue the policies of his father. At first, Alexander considered peace negotiations as humiliating for Russia, but would later buckle under the influence of his Foreign Minister, Karl Nesselrode. Due to this, the new Russian Emperor accepted negotiations, increasing the possibility of finding a mutual diplomatic solution to the war. In the middle of March, a new peace conference in Vienna began, between the emissaries of France, Great Britain, Russia, and Austria. The Russians accepted the negotiations on the basis of the previously mentioned Four Notes of Vienna. However, because the parties could not reach an agreement pertaining to the limitations on the Russian navy in the Black Sea, the peace conference was stopped in April of 1855.

By spring of 1855, it was clear that the Russian army was stretched out across a vast area, protecting the realm's many borders. Some half a million troops were deemed necessary to maintain order within the Russian Empire, some 260,000 were guarding the coasts of the Baltic Sea, around 293,000 soldiers were positioned in Poland and Western Ukraine – out of fears of an Austrian invasion, 121,000 troops were in Bessarabia and along the Black Sea coast, 183,000 men were stationed at the Caucasus front, while the Crimean peninsula only had 60,000 troops left. In comparison, the Allied forces had – by April – had around 224,000 troops at their disposal in the battlefields, of which 120,000 were French troops, 32,000 British, and 55,000 Ottomans. Some 15,000 troops of the Kingdom of Sardinia, commanded by General Alfonso la Marmora, also joined the allied cause.

Casualties were high too. Not counting those perished from diseases and malnutrition, the Russians – by the end of April 1855 – had twice as many casualties as the allies. Their wounded were hospitalized in the great field hospital that was erected close to Belbek, some six kilometers out of Sevastopol. The Russians also lost some competent commanders: the famed engineer Eduard Totleban was critically wounded and retired, while the able Pavel Nakhimov was killed in action. Furthermore, after the Allied occupation of Kerch and the blocking of the supply routes through the Azov Sea, the Russians began feeling the serious setbacks, lacking ammunition and equipment. In comparison, the allies – thanks to their developed industries – reached a never before seen concentration of weaponry and a tempo of industrial manufacture. The Russians, whose economy was still largely based on serfdom, could not compete in this regard.

To that end, the Siege of Sevastopol was turning into a true disaster, a drawn out siege under the worst of conditions. Lacking ammunition, food, water, and winter equipment, the Russian General Gorchakov began preparing for an evacuation to the northern part of the

Sevastopol bay. Most of the local populace, lacking food and water and fearing the outbreak of an epidemic, already abandoned the city. One of the eyewitness accounts from the time describes Sevastopol as the "city that is more akin to a graveyard". The dire conditions and the situation were described in detail by the famed Russian writer, Leo Tolstoy, in his work, the "Sevastopol Sketches". Many soldiers also resorted to desertion, due to a lack of food. Rumors began circulating that a revolt of the soldiers was inevitable. All of this came as a stark reminder for the Russian command that the siege was not going to last much longer. The Emperor Alexander II began searching for a chance to end the war in a way that was acceptable for the Russian pride. This could be achieved with a military achievement (a victory in battle) that could serve as a start of new peace negotiations with the French and the British, this time from a better position for the Russians. To that end, the Emperor ordered commander Gorchakov to make one last try to break the siege, emphasizing the importance of an offensive before the arrival of additional allied troops. Of course, most of the commanders greatly doubted the outcome of such an offensive, but the plan was nonetheless accepted, since it came from the Emperor. On August 9th, Gorchakov's plan was accepted: the Russians were to attack French and Sardinian positions on the Chernaya River.

The Battle of the Chernaya River ensued one day after the allied celebrations of the Assumption Day and the Feast Day of the Emperor of France. In the early morning of August 16th, the Russian forces attacked. Gorchakov hoped to use the element of surprise, especially due to the fog. He had at his disposal some 58,000 men, against just 28,000 men on the French and Sardinian side. However, even though he had numerical superiority, Gorchakov's troops were largely made up from fresh recruits and militia men. However, a number of deciding factors worked much to the failure of the Russians. Bad organization, bad directions by Gorchakov, and the lack of experienced soldiers all spelled doom for the offensive. The battle was often dubbed as a "massacre" of Russian soldiers. Disorganized and badly armed, the Russian infantry was sent across the Chernaya river without sufficient support, hoping to take the adjacent high ground. However, without any cavalry or cannon support, the soldiers suffered catastrophic casualties. In just around 20 minutes, some 2,000 Russian soldiers were dead. The battle ended as a total disaster for the Russians, and the last chance for breaking the siege on the ground was lost. The battle also put in the question the capabilities of the Russian army at that point: even with immense numerical superiority, the battle ended in utter defeat, with five times as many casualties as the enemy. Furthermore, Emperor Alexander lost his chance to end the war on favorable terms, which he hoped to gain with victory in this battle. But those that suffered the most were the common Russian soldiers. The battle was a great slaughter of men, and that caused the common soldiers to lose faith in their commanders. It was now only a question of time before the Siege of Sevastopol would end in total defeat.

Realizing the hopelessness of their situation, the Russians began their final preparations of evacuating Sevastopol. This plan consisted of crossing the bay from the souther to the northern side, from the fortress of Nicholas to the fortress of Michael. For this task, the engineers had to construct a pontoon bridge that was 960 meters long, and for whose building they used wood which had to be brought from as far as 300 kilometers away. Still, with around the clock work, the bridge was completed on August 27th. The allies, in the meantime, questioned numerous Russian deserters, acquiring substantial information about their enemy's situation. They were well aware that the Russian defense of Sevastopol wouldn't last too long. After all, the result of the siege depended entirely on the supplies of ammunition and weapons – and Russia was unable to provide the quantity of these that would match the allies. This fact greatly affected the development of the situation.

The next crucial event of the Siege of Sevastopol was centered on the outlying fortress of Malakoff. This was one of the defining, culminating events of the whole Crimean War, and one of the fierces clashes as well. Malakoff redoubt was one of the fortifications designed to defend the approach to the Sevastopol, and was situated some 4 kilometers (2.5 miles) outside of the city itself. In the months preceding the Battle of Malakoff, the area around Sevastopol was turned into a true and ominous foreshadowing of the debilitating trench warfare of the First World War. An area constantly ravaged by mutual bombardment, criss-crossed by entrenchments and makeshift fortifications, muddy and devastated, the Siege of Sevastopol was turning into a hell on earth. And with the Russian attempts to break the siege failed, the allies knew that it was time for one final assault. At Malakoff, it was the French that took the lead. Their attack was preceded by vicious bombardment, which gave the French commander, Marshal Pelissier, the utmost confidence in the victorious outcome of the battle. Around noon, on September 8th 1855, the French began their assault, abruptly attacking along the right sector of the siege lines, at Malakoff. The ensuing fight was some of the most vicious and brutal in the entire war. In a defining moment of the battle – and the war itself – one of the French *zouaves*, Eugene Libaut, reached the top of the Malakoff redoubt and raised proudly the French flag. The battle was an allied win, and the Russians were defeated. The loss of Malakoff meant also the loss of Sevastopol. The numbers in this battle were an all-time high too: the French fielded 70,500 troops, facing 59,500 Russians. The former had 10,000 casualties, while the latter had 13,000.

At the same time – on the same day – the British launched the attack on the opposite flank, at the Battle of the Great Redan. Casualties were high, and the clash ended with the attack repulsed, leaving the Russians victorious. However, Malakoff redoubt was a much more important strategic position, and its capture by the French dictated the fate of

Sevastopol. When the Russians realized that the Great Redan which they defended couldn't be defended or held because Malakoff fell, they promptly blew up their magazine stores, and evacuated the whole of Sevastopol. Even though Malakoff was a smaller redoubt, it overlooked the whole city and had great strategic importance. From this point, the French could bombard any point in the city, and virtually had control of it. Knowing this, the Russians finally suffered defeat in the Siege of Sevastopol. Destroying equipment and vital supplies, they abandoned their defenses and began an evacuation across the pontoon bridge. This evacuation lasted a full thirteen hours. Several great fires raged through the city, some burning for several days. When the allied troops finally entered the contested city of Sevastopol, they saw utter despair and destruction. Any city that is besieged would be a miserable place, but Sevastopol in 1855 was something truly horrifying. The "Times" correspondent, William Russell, was amongst the first to enter the conquered city, and what he saw was akin to hell on earth. He wrote of disturbing scenes of wounded and dying soldiers left without water or food, in pain and filth, to the mercy of the invading allied troops.

"Inside the sight was too terrible to dwell upon. The French were carrying away their own and the Russian wounded, and four distinct piles of dead were formed to clear the way. The ground was marked by pools of blood, and the smell was noisome; swarms of flies settled on dead and dying; broken muskets, torn clothes, caps, shakos, swords, bayonets, bags of bread, canteens, and haversacks, were lying in indescribable confusion all over the place, mingled with heaps of shot, of grape, bits of shell, cartridges, case and canister, loose powder, official papers, and cooking tins.[...] The ditch outside, towards the north, was full of French and Russians, piled over each other in horrid confusion. On the right, towards the Little Redan, the ground was literally strewn with bodies as thick as they could lie, and in the ditch they were piled over each other. Here the French, victorious in the Malakoff, met with a heavy loss and a series of severe repulses. The Russians lay inside the work in heaps, like carcases in a

butcher's cart; and the wounds, the blood—the sight exceeded all I had hitherto witnessed.[...]

Descending from the Malakoff, we came upon a suburb of ruined houses open to the sea—it was filled with dead. The Russians had crept away into holes and corners in every house, to die like poisoned rats; artillery horses, with their entrails torn open by shot, were stretched all over the space at the back of the Malakoff, marking the place where the Russians moved up their last column to retake it under the cover of a heavy field battery. Every house, the church, some public buildings, sentry-boxes—all alike were broken and riddled by cannon and mortar. [...]

Of all the pictures of the horrors of war which have ever been presented to the world, the hospital of Sebastopol offered the most horrible, heartrending, and revolting. How the poor human body could be mutilated, and yet hold its soul within it, when every limb is shattered, and every vein and artery is pouring out the life-stream, one might study there at every step, and at the same time wonder how little will kill! [...] Entering one of these doors, I beheld such a sight as few men, thank God, have ever witnessed. In a long, low room, supported by square pillars arched at the top, and dimly lighted through shattered and unglazed window-frames, lay the wounded Russians, who had been abandoned to our mercies by their General. The wounded, did I say? No, but the dead—the rotten and festering corpses of the soldiers, who were left to die in their extreme agony, untended, uncared for, packed as close as they could be stowed, some on the floor, others on wretched trestles and bedsteads, or pallets of straw, sopped and saturated with blood, which oozed and trickled through upon the floor, mingling with the droppings of corruption. [...]

Many, nearly mad by the scene around them, or seeking escape from it in their extremest agony, had rolled away under the beds, and glared out on the heart-stricken spectator—oh! with such looks! Many, with legs and arms broken and twisted, the jagged splinters sticking through the raw flesh, implored aid, water, food, or pity, or, deprived of speech by the approach of death, or by dreadful injuries in the head or trunk, pointed to the lethal spot."

Fates Decided in the Caucasus: The Siege of Kars

In the meantime, the front at the Caucasus was vaning – but it still had one last major action in store. Up to May 1855, disease, malnutrition, and inhuman conditions have decimated the Ottoman forces in the east. From some 120,000 troops, only 75,000 remained fit for action. And for the Ottomans , the situation was not going to improve. Their Caucasus armies, stationed in the fortresses of Kars, Batum, and Erzurum, spent the winter of 1854-1855 in extremely unhealthy conditions. Numerous reports and letters survive from the time that point to the inhuman conditions that these soldiers had to endure. Food was scarce and malnutrition rampant, clothing was poor and unfitting for the season, and the troops were crammed in poorly ventilated, ill-heated, and overcrowded accommodations. These were conditions ideal for the spread of illness and contagious diseases such as typhus. Due to these circumstances, well over 20,000 men perished from poor conditions. A report from as early as March 1854 states that of 17,000 troops that were based in Kars, 11,000 were in the hospitals.

Another burdening factor for the Ottomans in the Caucasus region was the enmity with many native ethnicities. The foremost were, of course, the local Armenian populace. They kept the Russians, commanded by General Nikolay Muravyev, well-informed about the Ottoman positions and conditions within Kars. Thanks to this information, the Russian command judged that the contingent within the fortress had some five months worth of supplies. To that end, it was decided that a siege, which would starve the garrison out, was the best choice. What ensued was the Siege of Kars, the last major operation of the entire Crimean War. Originally, Emperor Alexander II, continuing the war his father begun, sought a way to lift the pressure away from the besieged Sevastopol on Crimea. To that end, he ordered General

Muravyov to shift focus and lead the troops stationed in the Caucasus against the crucial Ottoman positions in the region of Asia Minor. Following these orders, Nikolay Muravyov combined the smaller contingents of his army into a single, stronger army that numbered some 25,700 soldiers and 96 cannons. And it was Muravyov that decided it was Kars he needed to take – the most important of all Ottoman fortresses in Anatolia. However, the British had a say in the matter as well. Sometime in late 1854, the British had sent General William Williams, a seasoned commander of Canadian origins, to Kars with the intent to assess the overall situation with their Ottoman allies, and to report directly to Lord Raglan, the then commander-in-chief of the British forces in Crimea. What William Williams had to report was not ideal. The Ottoman forces were in a dire state: the city of Kars was utterly deplorable, and the Ottoman army was full of fresh recruits. To make matters worse, their weaponry was quite outdated, and the men hadn't received *any* payment in months. A medical system was non-existent – no field hospitals existed at all. Ottoman senior officers and commanders weren't even present at Kars, but lived in Istanbul at the time. All of this caused an immensely low morale amongst the Ottomans, and made desertion commonplace. It thus fell upon General Williams to address the situation, and make these men ready to fight the oncoming Russians. To that end, he took command of Kars and its forces, alongside several foreign officers. Together, they busily worked on reinforcing the defenses of Kars, inspiring the troops and raising morale. Discipline was also important, and rigorous training that would bring the raw recruits up to the standard of the day. It was a great challenge, and the work was incessant. And Williams succeeded: by springtime of 1855, the fortress of Kars was ready to defend itself, with 17,000 strengthened troops within.

Before beginning the siege proper, the Russians decided for an attack. However, the assault was repulsed by the Ottomans commanded by Williams. The renewed vigor and the ferocity of the Ottoman garrison came as a surprise for the Russians. Muravyev nevertheless pushed a second assault, which was this time a success. The Ottomans remained in Kars, and the Russians took possession of the main road and the heights over the city. This was an excellent position for a prolonged siege, a thing that Muravyev recognized and accepted. He changed tactics and began a long siege with the intent to starve the Ottomans out. The siege proceeded well from June until September, when Muravyov received news of the misfortune and the fall of Sevastopol. Furthermore, the Ottoman commander, Omar Pasha, desperately sought to relieve Kars. To that end, he left Sevastopol with some 45,000 soldiers, landing north of Kars, at Sukhumi, on September 6th. This was a whole new situation, one that Muravyov did not count on. Due to this, he changed his tactics and decided for an all out attack. This was a third assault, launched on September 29th. It was also the fierces one: the Russians fought desperately to gain control of the fortress, fighting bitterly for seven hours with no success. The Ottomans, bolstered by

William Williams, persevered and held out, knowing that help from Omar Pasha was on its way. Alas, Omar Pasha would never reach Kars. His plans changed, and he remained in the region of Mingrelia around Sukhumi, warring there instead. And with the winter coming in, journeying to Kars was risky. This meant that William Williams and his gallant Ottoman troops were, in the end, left alone to fend for themselves, isolated and very short on supplies. Their isolation was even more certain with the onset of October, as heavy snows made their isolation all the more definite. The Russians, however, continued their siege even after their assault was repulsed.

Towards the south, another Ottoman army landed, this time in the city of Trebizond. This army was commanded by Selim Pasha, whose task was to march towards Erzerum, where he was to prevent the Russians from penetrating further into Anatolia. Muravyev responded to this new threat by sending a part of his army from the Kars siege to meet Selim Pasha head on. This contigent was successful, and the Ottomans were seemingly defeated at the small Battle of Ingur River on November 6th, 1855. Reports are at odds, and it is likely that the battle was indecisive.

By that point, winter was already in full swing. Remaining at Kars would mean certain suicide for General William Williams and the Ottoman garrison. To that end, Kars officially surrendered to the Russian commander Muravyov, on November 28th, 1855. The siege lasted several months, and even though assaults were all repelled, starvation could not be endured. Upon entering the conquered city, the Russians were horrified at what they saw. Reports of eye witnesses state that the Ottoman soldiers were heaped in masses, *"too weak to be evacuated, and many of them in the throes of death."*

Undoubtedly, the true hero of the Siege of Kars was General William Fenwick Williams. The man took the task of defending Kars with a true passion and dedication. He connected with the Ottoman men and made their cause his own also, instilling hope back into their hearts. To the very last moment he shared in their sufferings, doing his best to save the city from conquest. Even when he knew that there won't be any aid or supplies from Istanbul or elsewhere, Williams remained steadfast in his efforts. When surrendering, he famously said that his Ottoman troops *"fell dead at their posts, in the tents, and throughout the camp, as brave men should who cling to their duty through the slightest glimmering of hope of saving a place entrusted to their custody".* The victorious Russian commander Muravyev was also fascinated by Williams. The defense he put up was so honorable and inspiring, that Muravyev treated his enemy with utmost respect. He stated upon meeting him: *"General Williams, you have made yourself a name in history, and posterity will stand amazed at the endurance, courage and the discipline which the siege has called forth in the remains of the army."*

William Williams was captured and taken to the Russian city of Ryazan, where he was treated very well and with all honors, and he even got to meet Emperor Alexander II before returning back to his home.

All in all, the Siege of Kars was one of the final events of the Crimean War, and one of the costliest operations in the Caucasus theater of war. It lasted from early June to late November 1855, and saw the Russian force of 25,700 men, facing a garrison of 17,000 Ottomans. But when the siege ended, the Russians had 6,500 casualties, while the defenders of Kars had catastrophic losses: 2,300 dead, and 5,000 wounded. It was a horrifying and costly culmination of the Crimean War.

Some attention needs to be directed to the events that transpired during this time in Georgia, and its coastlines that were a strategic spot on the Black Sea edge. While Kars was under siege by the Russians, Omar Pasha was eager to leave the Siege of Sevastopol and to land his army in Georgia. Repeatedly he implored the western allies in Crimea to allow him leave, but the proposal was repeatedly vetoed. Omar Pasha Latas urged them of the dangers in store for Kars, but to no avail. At last the allies relented in August, granting him leave to land at Georgia. But by then, the perfect time for a campaign was lost. Yet even so, Omar Pasha landed in Georgia in September, with a contingent of several thousand men. First arriving in the port city of Batum, the Ottoman army had to march southwards for a 100 miles in order to reach Sukhum Kale fort. It was a show of force, a military maneuver that was meant to strike fear in the Russians and their general Muravyov, forcing them to lift the siege. However, Muravyov did not feel threatened. He did, nevertheless, feel enough pressure to launch a third and final assault onto Kars. His attempt was brutally repelled by the desperate defenders in the fort. But even with the defeat in the assault, Muravyov kept up with the siege, knowing that Omar Pasha would not arrive. Winter was ongoing, and the chance was lost for Kars to be reinforced. Those in Kars knew that *"all luck depended on whether*

Muravyov would be scared or not". When this did not happen, everyone knew that Kars was lost. The surrender of the city followed soon after, in November.

An Overshadowed Theater of War: The Baltic Operations

The vicious battlefields of the Crimean War were not affixed only to the land, and only to the territories of the Ottoman Empire and Crimea, that we already mentioned in detail. Much of the action was fought at sea, and in the areas of Europe and Asia that are often overlooked in modern historiography. When talking of the Crimean War, many go straight for the great battles of Balaclava, Inkerman, Sevastopol, and so forth. But when we shift our gaze elsewhere, we can see that death and warfare have reached far across the world, and became the insoluble part of the Crimean War as a whole. One of these "forgotten" theaters of war was at the Baltic Sea. The events that were much more dramatic and significant in the Crimean War have largely overshadowed the actions that happened at the Baltic. Most notable was a naval campaign of the Western allies, which occurred in this region and quite close to Saint Petersburg, the then capital of the Russian Empire. The allies laid great hopes in this campaign, where a powerful British Baltic Fleet under the command of Vice Admiral James Whitley Dundas had a plan to seize the fortresses of Kronstadt and Sveaborg. Doing so would – after a plan by Napoleon III – instigate Sweden to join the allies in their war against Russia, and would also threaten Saint Petersburg. And in order to further blockade Russian maritime trading, the British fleets would go on to ravage a series of Russian coastal trading posts and towns.

In April 1854, the combined Anglo-French fleet sailed into the Baltic, with the aim to attack Kronstadt, the important Russian naval base, and the place where the Russian fleet was stationed. Leading the British was Charles Napier, a seasoned naval commander, while the French were led by Alexandre Deschenes. This combined fleet was powerful on paper, but in reality it had many shortcomings: most of the seamen lacked crucial experience, the ships were unsuited for actions in the frigid Baltic, and the crews were undermanned. Yet even so, the fleet was powerful enough to instill fear into the Russians: their ships never left their moorings. Charles Napier succeeded in reconnoitering many crucial locations, penetrating as deep as the Gulf of Finland.

In August of 1854, the Allied fleet returned to Kronstadt to attempt another assault, but there was no success – the Russian fleet patrolled in a confined area around the fortress. Similarly, the Baltic fleet did not engage the fortress of Sveaborg. Even though Napier and Deschenes had joint command of the largest naval fleet assembled since the Napoleonic Wars, they still considered Sveaborg too strongly fortified. Success was not probable. For this reason, only minor bombardment was conducted of the Russian coastal batteries, in 1854 and 1855. Furthermore, the fleet succeeded in blockading Russian commerce in the Gulf of Finland. The blockade proved an overall success for the allies, since the Russian Empire depended greatly on its imports from the sea. Both the supplies for the military engaged in the Crimean War, and the domestic economy were affected greatly by the allied blockade. Due to this, Russia had to conduct imports from Prussia, which were overland and much more expensive due to this. Historians agree that the naval blockade helped shorten the Crimean War, undermining the Russian economy. However, the blockade did face criticism internationally, since the allies did inflict substantial naval damage by burning tar warehouses along the coast, as well as ships. Some considered that the burning of coastal stores and settlements was an attack on innocents, even though Britain and Russia were in a state of war. The comments were deemed confusing at best. For example, in London the Member of the Parliament, Thomas Gibson sought in the House of Commons, from the First Lord of the Admiralty an explanation of *"a system which carried on a great war by plundering and destroying the property of defenseless villagers"*. But in all actuality, all actions within the Baltic Sea were in accordance with the laws of war, and in the nature of binding forces. The British understood quite well the importance of diverting Russian attention from the south and from Crimea. But more importantly, the Baltic theater of war was a way to keep a great number of Russian soldiers "occupied" and protect Saint Petersburg, i.e. not to allow the Russian emperor to shift those troops to Crimea. And the plan worked.

Interestingly, in their actions against the Russians in the Baltic, the British and the French waged war mostly against the Finns. How so? Acting in the Baltic, the British mostly dealt damage to Finland (Grand Duchy of Finland at the time) and its territories, since a very large part of the merchant fleet that sailed under the Russian flag was located in Finland, a Grand Duchy that was under the control of the Russian Empire since 1809. Due to this, the conflicts that ensued against Finland are commonly called in historiography (and in Finland) as the Åland War, since the majority of the action occurred in and around the archipelago of Åland, off the coast of Finland. However, this war also encompases the conflicts that happened beyond the Åland Islands, in the Gulf of Bothnia itself, and the Gulf of Finland. Numerous raids and attacks happened during this conflict, such as the attack on the Hogland island in the Gulf of Finland, clashes in the Turku archipelago, and several raids on less fortified targets on the Finnish coast itself.

The Åland War constitutes a major part of the Crimean War as a whole, and is centered almost exclusively on naval warfare and naval raids conducted by the British and the French. In the spring of 1854, the British fleet, commanded by Sir Charles Napier, and the French fleet, commanded by Vice Admiral Deschernes, sailed into the Finnish waters. Together, they commanded a force of 80 ships and some 43,000 men. And soon enough, action began. In the harbors of *Raahe* and *Oulu*, great damage was inflicted: tar supplies, stocks of wood and wooden equipment, and the shipyards were all set ablaze. Next was a clash at *Kokkola*, where the enemy ships were badly beaten and sent fleeing. Reports state that after the war, the total loss for the Finnish fleet was more than 77,000 tons, while the British seized some 28,500 tons of shipping.

Arguably the most important event of the Åland War was the attack on the Russian fortress of Bomarsund, located on the Åland Islands.

A new, 19th century fortress, Bomarsund was not yet finished by the outbreak of the Crimean War. The construction began in 1832 by Russia, on the strategic location of Sund, in the Åland islands. The original plan was quite grand, with 12 subsidiary towers arranged in a semicircle. However, only 2 of these towers were fully built by the time the British arrived. This left it still very much vulnerable from overland attacks. In case of naval attacks, it was deemed that the narrow passages around the fortress wouldn't be navigable by sailing ships. This was partially true, but the more modern steam ships did not have those difficulties, making Bomarsund vulnerable from the sea as well. The first attack on Bomarsund occurred on June 21st 1854. Three ships of the British fleet bombarded the fortress, but were met with a response from the enemy artillery. This skirmish was short and indecisive, and both sides suffered light casualties. Interestingly, this first assault on Bomarsund is recorded in history as the event that precipitated the first ever Victoria Cross award in history! The award was granted to one Charles Davis Lucas, a seaman who showed great bravery in the face of danger. At the height of the battle at Bomarsund, a live artillery shell landed on the British ship on which Lucas was present. Everyone ducked for cover awaiting the blast, but Lucas bravely tossed the shell into the sea, saving the ship and his fighting mates.

And even the first assault was indecisive, the British returned for a second try. Near the end of July 1854, some 25 ships of the British fleet sailed into the Bomarsund waters and surrounded the fortress.

This time, a different approach was taken. The British now knew that it won't be possible to capture Bomarsund by a naval attack only. To that end, they waited patiently in the waters for the French ground troops to arrive and attack simultaneously. In response, realizing the plan, the Russian forces employed a scorched earth policy, destroying the surrounding countryside in an effort to dissuade the enemy from continuing with the supposed siege of the fortress. Nevertheless, the attack on Bomarsund occurred. On August 8th 1954, the French infantry arrived: some 7,000 eager and able soldiers landed to the south of the Bomarsund fort, with an additional 2,900 French and British troops landing to the North of it. On august 10th, they were joined with the artillery squadrons that were positioned on a hilly, raised ground. The assault proper began only three days later, on August 13th, when the French artillery batteries opened fire on one of the Bomarsund towers. Near the end of the day, the artillery succeeded in suppressing the enemy defending the tower, allowing the French infantry to effectively assault it. In return, the Russian defenders promptly withdrew, but did not want to leave the strategically important tower in French hands. To that end, they left a small crew to store gunpowder and totally destroy the tower, but the French prevented them, capturing the site intact. The Battle of Bomarsund continued in earnest, and by August 15th, the roles were somewhat reversed: the Russian artillery now pounded the French positions, scoring a bullseye hit on the gunpowder magazines in the lost tower and creating an immense explosion that totally demolished it. With this outlying tower out of the way, however, the allies could proceed with the main assault on Bomarsund itself. This began on August 15th, late in the day, with the combined land and naval artillery opening devastating fire on the fortress. And when the British land cannons joined in the barrage, the allies managed to destroy the second tower as well. At this point, the Russians hoped that the bombardment would stop and a land attack would occur, but the allies knew better: they decided to pummel the Bomarsund fort with devastating artillery barrages, which continued for hours on end. Eventually, the barrage created a huge gaping hole in one of the fortress walls, and most of the Russian guns were knocked out. With no way out of the situation, the Russian commander formally surrendered Bomarsund to the allies on August 16th 1854. The battle saw some 32,000 French and British troops attacking the garrison of roughly 3,000 Russian (Åland) troops. The former suffered 85 casualties, and the latter had 53, and an additional 2,000 taken captive. This was one of the costliest and most destructive clashes in the so-called Åland War.

After capturing Bomarsund, the allies decided that the best course of action was to completely demolish it, and thus knock out of the "game" one of the major Russian forts in the Baltic. The process of destruction went on for several months, and some 700,000 bricks from the ruins were later shipped out to Helsinki and used in the construction of the Orthodox Uspenski Cathedral there.

An interesting event occurred after the Battle of Bomarsund, where 300 Finnish grenadiers were captured by the British. These men were transported to England, and were imprisoned at Lewes in East Sussex. Most of the soldiers were Finnish, with just a few officers being Russian. In Lewes, the prisoners gained quite a fame, and were loved by the local citizens. They were allowed to create toys and earn money, and they became a proper tourist attraction. Their handiwork earned them up to 3,500 pounds in today's money – per day! This, alongside their fame and popularity, caused quite a scandal in England, considering that young Englishmen were dying in Crimea, and the Finnish prisoners of war were earning considerable money, wearing gold jewelry, and being pampered far and wide. After a brief revolt by these prisoners of war, a number of them were imprisoned in harsher conditions in Sheerness, where 28 of them would die from poor conditions and tuberculosis.

Today, a memorial monument stands in Lewes, in memory of these Finnish men that died while prisoners of war. A popular ballad was penned by the surviving prisoners, known today as the War of Åland (Finnish: *"Oolannin sota"*, Swedish: *"Det Åländska kriget"*).

Another considerable event in the Baltic occurred in August 1855, when the French and British fleets attempted to destroy the heavily fortified dockyards of the Russian port of Sveaborg, outside of Helsinki. This was known as the Battle of Suomenlinna (after it's Finnish name), the Battle of Viapori, and the Bombardment of Sveaborg. It was fought from 9th to 11th August 1855, and was a major part of the Åland War. Sveaborg was constructed in the 18th century, during the Swedish rule over Finland, and was originally known as the Fortress of Sveaborg (Swedish Fort). The Finns later renamed it as Suomenlinna or Viapori. Suomenlinna means roughly the "Castle of Finland". This referred to its great strategic position, close to the capital of Helsinki. This was the main defensive position of the Grand Duchy of Finland, and as such one of the major fortifications of the Russians in the Baltic. This made it a logical target for the French-British fleet. Still, by the onset of the Crimean War, much of the artillery installed in Sveaborg was of an older type, which made it obsolete for the standards of that war. Yet even so, the troops at Sveaborg were ready to defend themselves from an allied attack which they all expected. Following the events in 1854 and the destruction of Bomarsund, and assault on Sveaborg was all but imminent. However, the Sveaborg garrison was in a dire position. The main bulk of the Russian Baltic fleet was still blockaded and isolated around Kronstadt fortress near Saint Petersburg, and the numerous coastal raids and skirmishes with the British and the French in the Gulfs of Finland and Bothnia only made things worse.

When the time for battle came on August 6th 1855, the Allied Baltic Fleet appeared with 77 ships in force. Exploiting the obsoleteness of the Sveaborg guns, the Allies made their battle lines some 3 kilometers off shore. This meant that the Sveaborg guns had no effective range to do them harm, but their own ships could still bombard the fortress.

And so it was, that on August 9th 1855, a vicious cannonade began. The allies bombarded Sveaborg for 48 hours straight, with the defenders unable to strike back. For two days, more than 1000 cannons pummeled the Sveaborg fortress walls. Luckily, the allies were not as cruel as to fire upon the city of Helsinki itself, sparing it from unnecessary destruction and civilian lives. It is said that more than 20,000 shells were let loose on the fortress. Great damage was caused to the buildings within, and several direct hits were scored on gunpowder magazines, which created huge explosions. Nevertheless, almost miraculously, the defenders of Sveaborg persevered. Much of the troops there survived uninjured, and the sailors of the Russian 120-gun ship, "Rossiya", commanded by Captain Viktor Poplonsky, steadfastly defended the entrance into the Sveaborg harbor. The Russian batteries still survived in spite of all the shelling. This led to a stalemate: the allies were not able to fully destroy the Sveaborg batteries, and the Sveaborg batteries had no range to fire back. Afterwards, the allied naval guns stopped firing, and the Russians feared that they planned a ground invasion. Luckily for them, no such thing occurred: the British and French forces eventually withdrew from Sveaborg. The Battle of Sveaborg ended as indecisive, and the allies suffered some 250 dead and wounded. The Russian losses remain unknown.

Afterwards, the British did not lose hope, and their goal of conquering Sveaborg still remained. To that end, they proceeded to assemble a *massive* new fleet that numbered more than 350 gunboats and special mortar vessels. This was known as the *"Great Armament"*, one of the greatest fleets of its time, and a force that would undoubtedly reduce

Sveaborg to dust. However, this great fleet was never put into action, as the Crimean War came to an end before it could be used.

The Battle of Sveaborg, and the Åland War in general, were the testing ground for some revolutionary new military technologies that would later totally change naval warfare. For example, the Russians managed to resist the British attacks by using a wholly new invention at the time: *blockade mines*. Naval mining was only beginning to appear by that time, and much of it is attributed to an inventor and engineer, Immanuel Noble, a Swede residing in Russia. He was the father of Alfred Nobel, after whom the Nobel Prize is named. Immanuel Nobel was thus an instrumental asset in the Russian war effort, and was one of the first engineers to work with explosives such as gunpowder and nitroglycerin. An interesting report from the period confirms that these blockade mines were used in the Baltic operations of the Crimean War: *"Torpedo mines, if I may use this name given by Fulton to self-acting mines underwater, were among the novelties attempted by the Russians in their defences about Kronstadt and Sevastopol".*

Another interesting new naval military technology was developed by the British, and was supposed to be used in the planned attack on the main Russian naval base at Kronstadt in 1856. These were the special "armored floating batteries", i.e artillery batteries that floated on water. They were already used in the Black Sea campaigns, at Kinburn in 1855, where they proved instrumental in the attack. However, the planned campaign of 1856 against Kronstadt never occurred, as the war ended by then. The threat of such an attack was a contributing factor for the unfavorable peace negotiatons that the Russians had to accept.

Another largely forgotten theater of war that unfolded in the Crimean War was situated in the Far East of Russia, in the remote and frigid waters around the Kamchatka Peninsula. The most notable event of this theater was the Siege of Petropavlovsk, a major event that led to many casualties. The Allied fleets were concerned about the Russian Siberian flotilla, and the threat it posed for the French and British trade routes in the area. To that end, the allied ships stationed in the naval base of Callao in Peru, were instructed to wage war against Russian shipping and targets in the Pacific. There were three main Russian targets presented: the island of Novo-Arkhangelsk (modern-day Sitka in Alaska, US), Okhotsk, the largest Russian settlement on the Pacific coast, and Petropavlovsk, the major port city on the Kamchatka Peninsula.

The combined French and British fleet, commanded by Counter Admiral Auguste Febvrier Despointes and Rear Admiral David Price respectively, numbering 6 ships with 200 cannons and 1,700 men, descended firstly on Novo-Arkhangelsk, the capital of what was at the time "Russian America". No resistance was met here, and the island was quickly taken. Then the fleet proceeded to their next objective, Petropavlovsk.

On the Russian side was a seasoned Vice Admiral, Yevfimiy Putyatin, who had command of just two ships: a frigate with 44 guns, and another ship with 10 guns. Putyatin thus knew that he had no means to meet the allied fleets in open naval battle, or to effectively raid their trade routes. To that end, he decided the best course of action was to concentrate all his forces at Petropavlovsk, combining its garrison with the men from Okhotsk. In total, he had at his disposal around 1,000 soldiers, 67 cannons, and 2 ships.

On August 28th 1854, the Allies sailed into the Petropavlovsk bay, where they at once conducted reconnaissance. It was at once clear that the Russians were fortified and ready to defend themselves. The British commander for the action, Rear Admiral Price, decided for direct bombardment of the Russian coastal batteries, and ordered "reconnaissance-in-force" on the next day. Following the brief exchange of fire as a test of the Russian capabilities, Admiral Price came up with

a plan for the action. The attack was supposed to begin on August 30th, but oddly enough, Price was discovered in his cabin with a gunshot wound – self-inflicted. His apparent suicide was quite a mystery, and due to it, the attack was delayed 24 hours. The Russian commander Muravyov later wrote:

> *"... the English Admiral Price was killed in front of the Petropavlovsk port on his frigate and was buried in the Tarino Bay... Zavoiko in vain believed the captive's story that Admiral Price had allegedly shot himself. It was unheard of for a chief to shoot himself at the very beginning of a battle he hoped to win! Also Admiral Price could not accidentally shoot himself with his pistol. For what need did he could be take it in his hands, being on a frigate in a mile from our battery?.."*

Still, with the mystery unsolved, the attack on Petropavlovsk proceeded. The first attack was somewhat successful, although it ended as indecisive. The British ships successfully suppressed the Russian batteries, and received minor damage in return. After a while, a landing party successfully captured and spiked some of the Russian guns. Still, after the French frigate *Forte* signaled its wish to retreat, the allied ships withdrew from the assault.

On the next day, the French and British commanders were fiercely arguing about the next plan of attack. The French wanted to withdraw completely, while the British were eager to attack again. But in the end, the British prevailed, since the French admiral did not want his forces to seem cowardly. In the meantime, a land route was also discovered. The British sailed to the other side of the bay in order to bury their dead admiral Price. There they discovered American whalers living in tents, who told them that the Petropavlovsk was vulnerable from land, with a route that crested a hill. It was an ideal spot for an artillery attack from land, and the British were eager to use the chance given them.

To that end, the following plan of attack was assembled:

1. French naval column (200 French sailors from the ships Forte and Eurydice) – tasked to bring artillery up the hill from the north
2. Marine column (120 British and 80 French Marines) – tasked to seize the crest of the hill for the artillery from the north
3. British naval column (180 British sailors) – tasked with seizing and destroying Battery no. 5 and advancing into the town and turning to attack the hill from the east
4. Mixed naval column (120 British and French) – tasked with leaving a detachment to defend the beach and the landing craft and then advance along the beach and attack the hill from the west

Facing this force was the battered garrison of Petropavlovsk: some 920 men composed of officers, seamen, infantry, volunteers, and even the indigenous Kamchadal populace. What ensued was a ferocious fight, in which the Russians put up a stiff defense. And even though the Allies were numerically superior, the ensuing fight was marked by heavy casualties and their inability to penetrate Russian lines of defense. After just an hour or two, the Allies ordered a retreat, being unable to penetrate Petropavlovsk from the land. They had a total of 209 casualties, of which 52 were killed. On the other hand, the Russians had 37 killed and 78 wounded. The Siege of Petropavlovsk was a failure, even though everything pointed to it being a success. The Russians entrenched themselves and found favorable positions for defense, while the French showed numerous faults throughout the attack. And for the defenders, victory was a huge milestone, and effectively saved the

Russian possessions and presence in the Far East. The victory was dubbed a "ray of light among the dark clouds".

Nevertheless, Petropavlovsk was not kept: In April 1855, the Russian General Muravyov ordered a full retreat of its garrison, under the cover of snow. He was fully aware that the city and its defenses were unable to withstand another Allied assault which was incoming.

Other naval action in the area included the small allied landings on the far eastern islands of Sakhalin, and on Urup in the Kuril Islands. Further significant action occurred in the White Sea, beyond the Kola Peninsula. Here, in the autumn of 1854, a fleet of three British warships commanded by Sir Erasmus Ommaney left the Baltic region and sailed for the White Sea, where they conducted several raids and assaults. Notably, the squadron bombarded the coastal town of Novitska in August 1854, followed by the devastating bombardment and utter destruction of the coastal town of Kola, the oldest town on the Kola Peninsula. Ommaney's squadron successfully blockaded the major Russian port of Arkhangelsk, disrupting naval trade in the region. However, an attempt to assault and capture the city ended in failure. The fleet bombarded the town, while a landing party of 800 soldiers was repulsed. Still, a good deal of Russian properties along the coast were destroyed. Before these events, between 6th and 7th July 1854, the squadron conducted heavy bombardment of Solovetsky Monastery in the Onega Bay. After 9 hours of heavy cannonade, the squadron left without any gains.

The End of the Crimean War

Following the costly conquest of Sevastopol, the Crimean War was drawing to a much-coveted close. The war effort proved - in many ways – disastrous. The conditions in the heaviest zones of war were appalling at best, and great dissatisfaction with the conflict arose – both at home and on the front. This wave of displeasure was most acutely felt in Britain, where the public did not hide its growing dissatisfaction with the conduct of war. Reports of fiascos, scandals, embezzlement by the officers, devastating losses, disease and malnutrition, poor conduct and misinterpreted orders (The Charge of the Light Brigade), all contributed to this public outcry for the end of the war. To that end, a serious demonstration took place on Sunday, January 21st 1855, known popularly as the "Snowball Riot". Around 1,500 people gathered in protest at Trafalgar Square near "St. Martin-in-the-Fields", voicing their anger at the conduct of the war. As a sign of their displeasure, the protesters made snowballs and struck passing pedestrians, cars, buses, and cabs. This grew out of proportion, and the police intervened. However, they too received a "snowball attack", which compelled them to use their truncheons and to put down the riot in a more serious manner. This was obviously seen as a scandal that the British government did not need at all: the citizens were becoming quite displeased with the war and that was a serious matter.

The situation worsened within the Parliament. The Conservative party demanded that every soldier, sailor, and cavalryman that was sent to fight in the Crimean War be accounted for. Furthermore, they demanded a precise number of casualties sustained throughout the conflict. The Parliament passed a bill in favor of this investigation with a vote of 305 to 148. Soon after, the Prime Minister, George Hamilton-Gordon, Earl of Aberdeen resigned from his position of power on January 30th 1855. He was promptly replaced by Henry John Temple, Viscount Palmerston. Oddly enough, Palmerston adopted a policy of potentially continuing the war, wanting to once and for all end the Russian "threat to Europe". He proposed fomenting unrest within the Russian Empire, and stressed out that Prussia, Sweden and Norway were willing to join the allies' cause. What is more, it was no secret that Palmerston had no intent of ending the war. For him, the Crimean campaign was only the introduction to an even greater war that was directed at reducing the power of the vast Russian Empire. On September 25th 1855, he writes to Lord Clarendon as follows:

"It is the main and realistic goal of this war to contain the aggressive Russian ambitions. We went to war not to support the Sultan in Turkey, but to keep the Russians away from the Ottoman Empire. It is equally important for us to keep them away from Sweden and Norway as well."

The historian A. J. Taylor had a similar, realistic view of the state of things and the underlying British motives:

"The Crimean war was fought for the sake of Europe rather than for the Eastern question; it was fought against Russia, not in favour of Turkey.... The British fought Russia out of resentment and supposed that her defeat would strengthen the European Balance of Power".

However, the war mongering was not only exclusive to the British. The new Russian Emperor, Alexander II was not inclined to peace either, because a peace treaty was on unfavorable terms for Russia. Due to this, he prolonged his war efforts by besieging the citadel of Kars, hoping to divert the allies away from Sevastopol. Kars fell on November 29th 1855, and that gave the Russians control over more territories than the western allies. Alexander II considered that the conquest of Kars was enough of an achievement to give him the needed balance to the fall of Sevastopol. And with that, he decided to go on with the peace negotiations in Paris.

But the war mongering ideas of Palmerston were not met with approval. In the first place, France opposed them. This nation sent by far the most men into the yawning jaws of the Crimean War, and suffered an incredible number of casualties, just a few decades after the Napoleonic Wars stripped this country of its youth. To that end, they wanted the war to end, and were joined in this notion by Austria. France carried it on its shoulders the greater deal of the war effort, and was furthermore hampered by infectious diseases that ravaged its troops in the autumn and winter of 1855. Napoleon III was thus absolutely opposed to continuing the war, so he made efforts to end it without damaging his alliance with Great Britain, which was the cornerstone of his foreign politics.

The Austrians then sent an ultimatum to the Russians, urging them on accepting the peace negotiations based on the so-called "Four Notes of Vienna". There was also the present threat of Austrians joining the allies militarily, as well as the indications that Sweden was to join the cause as well. Back in Russia, Emperor Alexander II conducted a meeting of his top officials, whereupon they concluded that the Russian Empire had no more means to prolong the war. They also considered the very much real threat of a peasant rebellion, since this class always bore the brunt of every war. Alexander was fully aware that a continued war would push Austria, Prussia, and Sweden to join the war against them, and that national uprisings in Ukraine, Poland, and Finland were very much possible. To that end, he accepted the peace negotiations.

Due to this fact, the peace negotiations to end the Crimean War began soon after. They were conducted at the Congress of Paris in February 1856. They were surprisingly smooth – which was a stark paradox to the brutal and bloodthirsty war that raged on for the past three years. In the negotiations, the British and the Austrians had the harshest proposals and wants. Oddly enough, their ally, Napoleon III, did not support these proposals, since France had no particular interests in the Black Sea. Even so, the peace negotiations ended with the formal signing of the *Treaty of Paris* on March 30th 1856.

In accordance with the treaty, Russia was obliged to restore the Citadel of Kars, *"and all other parts of the Ottoman territory of which the Russian troops were in possession"*, to the Ottoman Empire. Furthermore, the Russians had to return the region of Southern Bessarabia to Moldavia. Next, the disputed Danubian Principalities of Wallachia and Moldavia were nominally returned to the Ottoman Empire, while the Austrians were forced to abandon their annexation of the same. This granted both Wallachia and Moldavia a degree of independence after centuries of Ottoman oppression.

Next, the allied powers – France, Britain, Sardinia, and the Ottoman Empire – had to restore to Russia *"the towns and ports of Sevastopol, Balaklava, Kamish, Eupatoria, Kerch, Jenikale, Kinburn as well as all other territories occupied by the allied troops"*. The Russian Emperor and the Ottoman Sultan then agreed *"not to establish any naval or military arsenal on the Black Sea coast".* The Russians were also prohibited from creating an armed fleet in the Black Sea. Due to this, the sea was opened to commerce and free sailing, just like Danube was. It was obvious that the Russians were the real losers in this war: every clause of the treaty that referred to the Black Sea was a loss to them, since it weakened their naval power and maritime trade, making them no longer a threat to the Ottoman Empire. The Russian ambitions were utterly defeated. In the end, the Treaty of Paris admitted the Ottoman Empire into the so-called "Concert of Europe" – a delicate balance of power amongst the major European powers. The Western Allies pledged to respect the territorial integrity and independence of the "Sick Man of Europe", the Ottoman Empire. The Ottomans too had to make some concessions. They agreed to make the causes of both their Muslim and Christian citizens of an equal rank. This did not work well for the radical Muslims within Istanbul, but it did work well to break the powerful Russian ideological weapon that focused on the oppressed Christian minorities. In the end, the real loser of the Crimean War was the Russian Empire. The British historian, Orlando Figes, perfectly sums it up:

> *"The demilitarization of the Black Sea was a major blow to Russia, which was no longer able to protect its vulnerable southern coastal frontier against the British or any other fleet... The destruction of the Russian Black Sea Fleet, Sevastopol and other naval docks was a humiliation. No compulsory disarmament had ever been imposed on a great power previously... The Allies did not really think that they were dealing with a European power in Russia. They regarded Russia as a semi-Asiatic state... In Russia itself, the Crimean defeat discredited the armed services and highlighted the need to modernize the country's defences, not just in the strictly military sense, but also through the building of railways, industrialization, sound finances and so on... The image many Russians had built up of their country – the biggest, richest*

and most powerful in the world – had suddenly been shattered. Russia's backwardness had been exposed....The Crimean disaster had exposed the shortcomings of every institution in Russia – not just the corruption and incompetence of the military command, the technological backwardness of the army and navy, or the inadequate roads and lack of railways that accounted for the chronic problems of supply, but the poor condition and illiteracy of the serfs who made up the armed forces, the inability of the serf economy to sustain a state of war against industrial powers, and the failures of autocracy itself."

Conclusion

The Crimean War was often dubbed a "medieval war in modern times". This was due to the sheer brutality and inhumanity that this brief war showcased. It was popularly stated that the Crimean War had never revealed a *"greater confusion of purpose"* but led to a conflict that stood out for its *"notoriously incompetent international butchery"*. But more importantly, this vicious clash is a perfect glimpse into the complexities of the ever-evolving political aims of the major powers of Europe. Arguably, at the center of this conflict was the frail Ottoman Empire. In the middle of the nineteenth century, the survival of this empire depended wholly on the balance of the other European powers, or the so-called "Concert of Europe". The regular wars with Russia (there were 12 Russo-Turkish wars in total), as well as the clear pretensions of Russia towards the conquest of the Ottoman territories, all greatly weakened the frail empire. On the other hand, the Russians were clearly dissatisfied with the unfavorable Dardanelles treaty of 1841, and the fresh pretensions of the new French Emperor Napoleon III. All of this affected the foreign policies of the Russian Emperor Nicholas II.

And when the notorious scandal over the rights of the Russian Emperor to protect the Orthodox Christians threatened the fragile balance of powers, the Russians were assured that the British and Austrians were remain loyal allies. This proved to be a wrong assurance. Napoleon III wanted prestige and affirmation of his new rule, as well as the support of the Catholic Church, while the British proved to be Russia's main rival in the power struggle in the Black Sea. Furthermore, the Austrians also failed to side with the Russian Empire, even though they were greatly indebted to them. They sought neutrality above all and feared an insurrection of the Slavic peoples in their empire, and thus took a mediating position, more on the side of the French and the British. On top of all of this, the Ottoman Sultan, Abdulmejid I, well aware of the rivalry between the western allies and the Russians, decided to take advantage and to reaffirm the Ottoman independence and national integrity. The tensions led to the conflicts in the Danubian Principalities, and the Crimean War was just a step away. In summary, the conflict was often dubbed as a true mess of causes, much of which were never well understood or explained. Russian ambitions of territorial expansion, the Ottoman struggle for survival, the desire of the French emperor to consolidate his rule, and the warmongering drive for prestige of the British – they all led to a war that was vicious, costly, and filled with mistakes and needless deaths.

According to some contemporary sources, the Russians suffered around 35,671 killed in action, 37,454 died of wounds, and around 377,000 died of disease. Other sources give somewhat lower numbers: 25,000 killed in action, 16,000 died of wounds, and 89,000 died of disease. The former numbers might be more accurate. On the other hand the allies suffered as well: The Ottomans had 10,100 killed in action, 10,800 died of wounds, and 24,500 died of disease. The British had 2,755 killed in action, 1,847 died of wounds, and 17,580 died of disease, and 18,280 wounded. The French suffered the most amongst the allied powers: They had 8,490 killed in action, 11,750 that died of wounds, 75,375 dead of disease, and 39,870 wounded.

But these are mere numbers. They cannot convey the sheer amount of suffering and pain that the poor soldiers – on all sides – had to endure. Death in combat or death from disease and starvation, the fate is undeserved no matter what. In many ways, the Crimean War was the last war of the "old school", the last war of grand battles and strategy, of line formations and the calm marching towards certain death. But however we look at it, we are able to see that it was filled with unnecessary death. Poor soldiers that fought for false ideals, giving their lives in utter misery for the machinations of pompous leaders seated on their thrones. Poor youth willing to die for the whim of an emperor: a whole generation taking its last dying breaths in mud and in water, ridden with disease and starving, for a cause they did not comprehend. And just like that, all their efforts – the sieges and the endless battles, were annulled, reversed, and made redundant with a simple peace treaty. Such is the nature of war, and the Crimean War was perhaps the most heartless and senseless of all.

References:

Badem, C. 2010. *The Ottoman Crimean War (1853-1856)*. BRILL.

Bancroft, J. 2016. *Echelon: The Light Brigade Action at Balaclava - A New Perspective*. History Press.

Bates, R. and Furneaux, H. and Massie, A. 2015. *Charting the Crimean War: Contexts, Nationhood, Afterlives*. Interdisciplinary Studies in the Long Nineteenth Century.

Copland, J. 2014. *Legacies of the Crimean War, 1854*. SA Medical Heritage Society.

Edgerton, R. B. 2000. *Death or Glory: The Legacy of the Crimean War*. Ingram Publisher Services, US.

Figes, O. 2012. *The Crimean War: A History*. Picador.

Grabar, G. K. 2017. *Krimski Rat*. Juraj Dobrila University of Pula.

Grant, J. 2013. *The Crimean War*. Pen & Sword Military.

Harris, S. M. 1999. *British Military Intelligence in the Crimean War, 1854-1856*. Psychology Press.

Holmio, A. K. E. 2001. *History of the Finns in Michigan*. Wayne State University Press.

Kinglake, A. W. 1868. *The Invasion of the Crimea: Battle of Balaclava*. W. Blackwood and Sons.

Kelly, C. 2008. *Mrs Duberly's War: Journal and Letters from the Crimea, 1854-6*. OUP Oxford.

Lambert, A. 2016. *The Crimean War: British Grand Strategy against Russia, 1853–56*. Routledge.

Peroš, I. *Krimski Rat*. Rostra.

Rath, A. C. 2011. *The Global Dimensions of Britain and France's Crimean War Naval Campaigns Against Russia, 1854-1856*. McGill University, Montreal.

Stikes, W. 2006. *Crimean War: The Diplomatic March to War to the Destruction of the Turks at Sinope*. La Grange.

Sulek, M. 2007. *The Last Romantic War: The Crimean War of 1854-1856 and The Genesis of Contemporary Wartime Humanitarian Relief*. ARNOVA.

Sweetman, J. 2014. *The Crimean War*. Routledge.

Tate, T. 2018. *A Short History of the Crimean War*. Bloomsbury Publishing.

Young, W. 2012. *Historiography of the Origins of the Crimean War*. International History.

Also by History Nerds

Celtic History
Ireland

Great Wars of the World
World War 1
World War 2
The Napoleonic Wars: One Shot at Glory
The Serbian Revolution: 1804-1835
Peace Won by the Saber: The Crimean War, 1853-1856
The Wars of the Roses

Irish Heroes
Grace O'Malley: The Pirate Queen of Ireland
William Butler Yeats: Nobel Prize Winning Poet
Scáthach
Finn McCool

The History of the Vikings

Vikings
Longships on Restless Seas

The Rise and Fall of Empires
Rome: The Rise and Fall

Standalone
The History of the United Kingdom
The History of Ireland
The History of America
Stalin
The Fiery Maelstrom of Freedom
The History of Scotland
Robert the Bruce
William Wallace: Scotland's Great Freedom Fighter
The History of Wales

Also by Aleksa Vučković

Great Wars of the World
Peace Won by the Saber: The Crimean War, 1853-1856